Animals of the Serengeti

and Ngorongoro Conservation Area

Adam Scott Kennedy
Vicki Kennedy

PRINCETON
press.princeton.edu

Published by Princeton University Press,
41 William Street, Princeton, New Jersey 08540
In the United Kingdom: Princeton University Press, 6 Oxford Street,
Woodstock, Oxfordshire OX20 1TW
nathist.press.princeton.edu

British Library Cataloging-in-Publication Data is available

Library of Congress Control Number 2013950248
ISBN 978-0-691-15908-9

Production and design by **WILD**Guides Ltd., Old Basing, Hampshire UK.
Printed in China

10 9 8 7 6 5 4 3

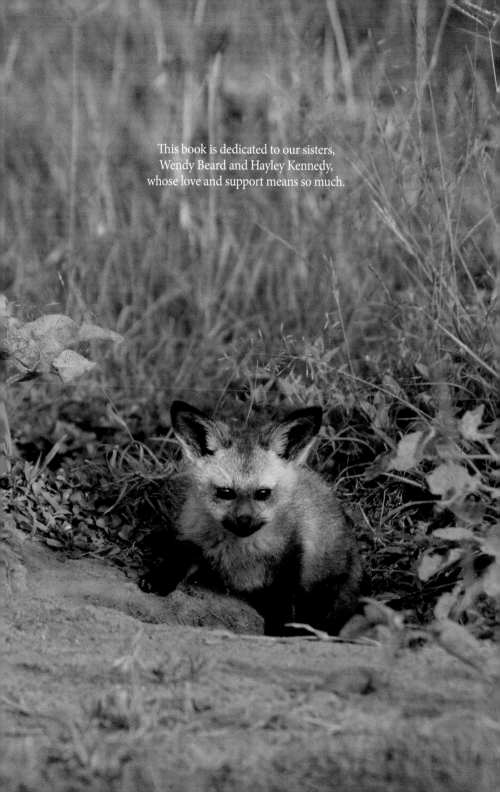

This book is dedicated to our sisters,
Wendy Beard and Hayley Kennedy,
whose love and support means so much.

Contents

About this book

The Serengeti – the Maasai term for 'land of the endless plains' – is world famous for the Great Wildebeest Migration that passes through each year, when vast numbers of these impressive beasts march on through the daily rigours of life. However, the 'Greater Serengeti area', including the famous Ngorongoro Conservation area, has so much more to offer the visitor than just Wildebeest, their menacing predators and the prospect of a kill. It is an incredibly beautiful area, diverse in habitats with a high number of species to entertain and observe. These range from the classic 'Big Five' species to smaller and more elusive mammals and reptiles that will delight visitors year round, time and time again. Watching wildlife can be as easy or as in-depth as you choose to make it. However, one thing is for sure, knowing what you are looking at and what behaviours to look out for can significantly enhance your safari experience.

One of the great things about mammals and reptiles is that we learn about them from a very young age; many of our first picture books taught us that E is for Elephant and Z is for Zebra, so we all have a head start when it comes to identifying animals. Most of us are enthralled by a multitude of wonderful TV documentaries that teach us even more about our favourite creatures and inspire us to travel across continents to observe them. Many visitors to the Serengeti arrive fully armed with a 'hit-list' of species they really must see, often having spent days undertaking the necessary homework before fulfilling their wildest animal dreams. And rightly so because safaris do not come cheap and getting the necessary time off work can take years of preparation. Maximizing your time and money should be a concern. Sometimes, however, this enthusiasm goes a little awry.

You might be surprised at the number of people expecting to see a Tiger in the Serengeti (we're sorry to burst your bubble if that includes you). And you really have to hear our Polar Bear story first-hand to believe it! But, on the whole, most visitors arrive properly prepared for 'Big Five' encounters and a whole lot more. To help you maximize your Serengeti safari experience, this photographic guide sets out with three major aims:

- to help you identify any species that you are not sure about (you know it is a mongoose – but which one?);
- to offer you lots of interesting and easily digestible information on each species; and
- to show you that there is so much more to look out for than just the 'Big Five'.

We want you to feel inspired by this book, to look beyond the usual and discover the unusual. We want you to have the confidence to make the right call on any animal you see. Don't just sit back and wait for your safari guide to tell you everything; pick up this book and tell them what you have just discovered – it makes for a greatly enriching experience.

If you're taking lunch at your camp or lodge and see a colourful lizard performing yoga before your very eyes, this book will not only tell you what it is, but also what it is doing and why!

Ultimately, we hope you find this field guide as useful as it is intended to be and enjoy it as much as we have enjoyed producing it.

SAFARI NJEMA!
(Good Safari!)

How to use this book

There are numerous guide books that cover the mammals and reptiles of the Serengeti, some of which we highly recommend (see *Further reading page 148*). However, from our own experiences of driving around the Serengeti National Park, the Ngorongoro Conservation Area and other wildlife-rich locations, we have found that most books suffer from some common drawbacks that lend themselves to becoming user-unfriendly, especially for the novice safari-goer. These typically include over-complex and baffling text, images so small that you need a magnifying glass to see what they are, or the coverage of species being so wide that many are not found in the region in which you are taking a safari.

For this reason we have adopted a simple approach to the illustrative plates in this book, combining large, clear images with an informative, but not exhaustive, text. Most importantly, though, this information relates only to the animals that are found within the 'Greater Serengeti area' which for the purposes of this book includes the Serengeti National Park, Ngorongoro Conservation Area (NCA), Ikorongo, Grumeti and Loliondo Game Controlled Areas, and Maswa Game Reserve. We hope you enjoy the layout of this book and would warmly welcome any feedback. It is worth pointing out here that we have decided not to include one large family of mammals within this guide – the bats. Although we love bats and their fascinating behaviours, we feel that getting a good view is difficult at the best of times and making a successful identification very challenging indeed.

The classification of species is an arbitrary business conducted by very scholarly people who change their collective minds from time to time, as shown in a recent decision to rename Africa's quintessential trees from *Acacia* to *Vachellia*. This was a highly contentious move that upset a lot of botanically-minded people in Africa, not to mention old romantics like us. So, as you will see, we have decided to ignore the latest thinking of these floracrats and have continued to use *Acacia* in the manner we are used to.

We have also chosen not to follow the strict scientific order of species followed by other texts (see *Further reading page 148*). Instead, the animals in this guide are shown in a simple order which we hope is straightforward to use. This order is reflected in the Contents page at the front of this book, should you need to refer to it quickly.

Throughout the book, we have sprinkled snippets of information on the latest scientific thinking about the animals, and fascinating facts about how some of our featured animals received their names. These should keep you entertained while waiting for a dozy Lion to wake up or an indecisive herd of Wildebeest to cross a river.

To help keep the book as concise as possible some shorthand has been adopted; the table opposite gives an overview of the terms used in each of the species accounts.

Common name	The name by which the animal is commonly known in English.
Scientific name	The name by which the animal is known scientifically, regardless of the local language. The names used follow those adopted by the International Union for Conservation of Nature (IUCN).
Swa:	The name by which the animal is commonly known in Kiswahili, the primary language of East Africa.
Maa:	The name by which the animal is commonly known in Maa, the language of the Maasai.
Size:	Two dimensions are given for most mammals, but only one for reptiles (these are in metres or centimetres and feet or inches): HBT = head, body and tail length (*i.e.* total length); SH = shoulder height (*i.e.* the height of the mammal at the shoulder).
Gestation:	The time spent in the womb from conception to delivery.
Recognition:	A simple and concise description of the animal to aid identification.
Habits:	A synopsis of the animal's behaviour including when it is active and what it does.
Where to find:	An indication of the habitats in which the species is likely to occur.
Feeds on:	The animal's diet.

Please note: These information boxes are tinted darker (*i.e.* this colour) for species that are primarily nocturnal.

Over the following pages, you will find some information that we hope will enrich your safari experience. First is a summary of the geography of the area covered by this book, so you can hold your own when talking about the landscape and habitats, followed by a map of the area. Among the features we are particularly proud to include within this guide are the top tips and comments from a selection of the very finest safari guides working in the Serengeti and NCA today – and it gives us great pleasure to introduce our 'Super Six' on *page 10*. This is followed by some background to the Great Migration and finally some of the best spots to watch wildlife and enjoy the landscape within the 'Greater Serengeti area' and the species you can expect to find there.

Finally, to help keep a record of the animals you see 'on safari', a small tick-box has been included next to each species description.

About the guides

There is no doubt that a great safari guide can make all the difference to your safari experience and, having had the privilege of working alongside many of the best guides in East Africa, we know that so much of their knowledge comes from their own experiences and is not just regurgitated from a text book. These guys and girls spend years in the field, observing rare behaviours that may seem impossible and experiencing exceptional encounters that sound implausible – but they are all real. It is because of our great admiration and respect for the professional guide that we wanted to include some of their experiences and wisdom within this book. They could all write exciting books of their own if they were not too busy showing their guests the wonders of life around their 'office', and so it is with great pleasure and pride that we present to you our 'Super Six' who have generously shared their thoughts, experiences and knowledge with us and you.

Albert Alfred Lucas

Born in Karatu district, just east of Ngorongoro Crater, Albert began guiding in 2001. This was a considerable departure from his tribal roots, as his Iraqw family are better known as fine farmers of the nearby lands. This energetic lifestyle comes through in Albert's work as he is usually the first guide out in the mornings and the last back in the afternoon to the Asilia camps where he now works. He relishes the challenge of finding Leopards, saying "It makes me happy to see how happy and excited my guests are, and that I have succeeded in finding them one of Africa's most elusive cats." The same goes for the elusive Black Rhino, of which Albert is a big fan: "we all need to make an effort to conserve these prehistoric animals." He relishes information-hungry guests and loves to be challenged on a subject. Albert is an expert on animal behaviour and ecology, and very knowledgeable on the region's geology.

Karipoi Kisirito Ngaiseri

Karipoi is a proud Maasai who was born in Ololosokwan, a village east of the northern Serengeti, and lives there today with his wives and children. After leaving school, Karipoi worked with his father as shepherd to the family's cows, goats and sheep and it was this time spent in the bush where he developed his passion for nature. He began work as a trainee chef at &Beyond's Klein's Camp in 2000 but dreamed of becoming a ranger. His company recognized his potential and now, after courses in English and guiding, he is a ranger with Serengeti Under Canvas, the mobile division of &Beyond. His favourite animal is the Leopard "they always look so well groomed and clean," he says.

Mudy (Mohammed) Nuru

Mudy hails from the Sandawe tribe, one of Tanzania's bushman tribes. With bush lore running in his blood, he has been a professional guide in East Africa since 1995. His passion for wildlife and observing it started at a young age when he would spend hours out in the bush exploring his surroundings. Mudy also has a special love for things bird-related and loves to get out on foot. He currently works at the stunning Ngorongoro Crater Lodge with &Beyond.

Patena Lukeine

Patena was born and raised in the Maasai village of Ololosokwan and he developed his love for nature and the great outdoors while looking after his cattle as a young man. He decided his true vocation was to study wildlife management in Arusha and, after working his way through the ranks in the hospitality industry, was selected for further career training with Asilia. He has eyes like a hawk and rarely misses a thing on his game-drives, professing a love for birds as well as mammals.

Patita Ole Maya

Working his way up from the shamba (vegetable garden) at Klein's Camp, Loliondo, Patita worked as a tracker for five years and has been a full-time guide for &Beyond since 2006. He loves walking safaris, as it reminds him of his explorative childhood, and his favourite animals are big cat cubs.

Titus Massay

Titus was born in Arusha and grew up at Karatu village just bordering with Ngorongoro Crater. He was always fond of fauna and flora while working with his grandfather's cattle, and was fortunate to be surrounded by the nature experts. He worked with the Crater Rhino project for 10 years before being selected into &Beyond's guide training scheme. His favourite animal is the Serval and he loves the way it hunts.

Geography of the Serengeti and Ngorongoro Conservation Area (NCA)

The Serengeti-Mara ecosystem covers an area of approximately 25,000 km² (9,600 square miles) and is defined academically by the area used by the Serengeti Wildebeest. Approximately 8,000 km² of the ecosystem lies in Kenya (Masai Mara and surrounds) but the majority is in Tanzania.

In the 'Greater Serengeti area', which includes the Ngorongoro Conservation Area (NCA), elevations above sea level (a.s.l.) vary greatly from the peaks of the Crater Highlands and Gol Mountains in the east (1,850 m / 6,070 ft a.s.l.) to the lowlands bordering the shores of Lake Victoria at Speke Bay (920 m / 3,020 ft a.s.l.). The lowlands get very hot in the dry season, affecting the availability of surface water and grass quality and resulting in the hordes of herbivores migrating to the relatively colder climes of the Masai Mara. This has not always been the case, however, since up until 1969 the migration into the Mara was not an annual event but only occurred in very dry years.

The bedrock of the region is incredibly old with a mix of Pre-Cambrian igneous and sedimentary rocks, and younger Tertiary and Quaternary volcanic features, including the Ngorongoro Crater, rising in the east close to the Great Rift Valley. Some of the most attractive geological features of the Serengeti are the granite inselbergs (German for 'island mountain') or kopjes (Dutch for 'little heads') that rise impressively out of the flat plains, such as the magical Simba Kopjes.

The fertile soils of the short grass plains were formed from volcanic ash released from multiple volcanic eruptions from nearby volcanoes, particularly *Ol Donyo Lengai* in the NCA. They sit on a hard layer of ash that is difficult for trees to permeate and so grasses prevail here. The soils of the north-east are nutrient poor and those to the west more suited to woodland, which have been susceptible to fire and elephant damage, in recent history.

Many of the clay-rich black cotton soils of the plains drain poorly, so not only does this result in some permanent swamps, such as Olbalbal Swamp in the shadow of the Ngorongoro Crater, surviving throughout the dry season, but also means that driving conditions can be treacherous after heavy rainfall. Much of the excess water finds its way into one of several well-defined rivers, including the Grumeti and Mbalageti, while most of the flow in the Mara River originates in Kenya.

Another important feature of the Serengeti is climate, especially rainfall. Although this differs markedly every year, on average two major periods of rainfall can be expected: the first 'short rains' in November and December, and the 'long rains' which are heaviest between March and May. Eventually, the cool, clear skies of the southern winter arrive, from mid-June to early October. Throughout the year, daytime temperatures are comfortably warm at between 28 °C and 38 °C (82–100 °F), while the night-time temperature rarely drops below 10 °C (50 °F). This combination of bedrock, soil type, drainage, slope and climate has created a wealth of conditions suitable for a wide variety of plant types.

Extensive grasslands are dominated by Red Oat Grass *Themeda triandra*, a staple for many herbivores in the Serengeti. These grasslands are kept open (*i.e.* mostly devoid of trees) because of the actions of so many herbivores rather than due to the soil conditions. The grassland is sometimes punctuated by an occasional Desert Date *Balanites aegyptiaca*, Sausage Tree *Kigelia africana* or Candelabra Tree *Euphorbia candelabrum*, although the latter seems to thrive on better-drained soils, especially on the slopes of the highlands. Along the major rivers, thicker tree cover is provided by Sycamore Fig *Ficus sycomorus*, Greenheart *Warburgia ugandensis* and Orange-leaved Croton *Croton dichogamus*, while the Yellow-barked Acacia *Acacia xanthophloea* appears to be more successful on smaller watercourses. Fantastic evergreen forests exist on the moist slopes of the Crater Highlands, especially on the rims of the smaller craters of Olmoti and Empakaai. Here you may encounter African Redwood *Hagenia abyssinica*, Onionwood *Cassipourea malosana* and African Wild Elder *Nuxia congesta* and large stands of African Bamboo *Arundinaria alpina*, while drives along the main Ngorongoro Crater road will reveal the mysterious Old Man's Beard or *Usnea* lichen that ripples on the moist breeze in the forest.

Grant's Gazelles in the Ngorongoro Conservation Area, with volcanic peaks to the east.

The great migrations

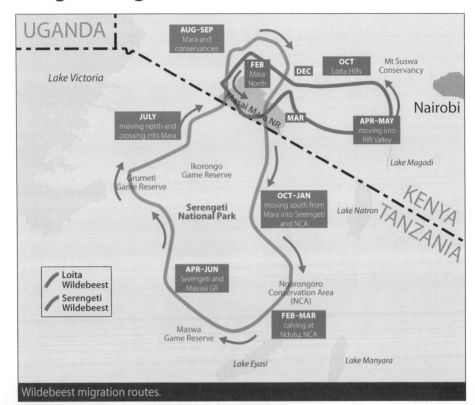

Wildebeest migration routes.

The prospect of an encounter with the largest mammal migration on Earth is what draws the majority of guests to the Serengeti – and rightly so. With over two million animals involved, consisting primarily of Wildebeest and Zebra, and a supporting cast of gazelle and other antelope species, the Great Migration is one of nature's greatest spectacles. Here we focus on the key species, the White-bearded Wildebeest, which starts its life and a continuous quest for fresh grass on the Ndutu Plains of the Ngorongoro Conservation Area and southern Serengeti in February and March.

The Serengeti Wildebeest is the smallest of the various subspecies and is also browner than the other subspecies, which are bluish or blackish. As explained in the Wildebeest description (*page 104*), the species typically migrates over 800 km in search of fresh green grass and fresh water. Although grass remains in the areas they have departed, the quality of the grass is the defining factor and reason for their continued movements. By mowing the grass and fertilising it with their dung and urine, the grasslands benefit from a net gain in nutrients that ensures good quality grazing when the herds return the following year.

As scientific research techniques continue to improve, we are learning more and more about the sensitivities of the herds to salt and mineral concentrations in particular. Phosphorus levels in the grass are now known to be very important to the movement of Wildebeest, and biologists hope to learn even more in the near future about how the herds are able to determine the levels of this crucial element. The current theory is that they achieve this is through hyper-sensitive taste glands. Other minerals can be detrimental to the animal's health if their concentrations are too high, especially in their drinking water, and it might be possible for the herds to taste dangerously high levels of certain elements and decide to move on.

A migration of a different kind
Following the Wildebeest on their migration is a fascinating species that benefits from the huge volume of dung left behind. Although the Dung Beetle is most often seen climbing over a pile of gnu poo, it is a capable flier and takes to the wing in order to keep up with its highly benevolent donors. At each stop, the beetle will roll a few dung balls and lay its eggs within, giving the emerging larvae a nutritious start in life before undergoing a metamorphosis into the winged adult beetle. There may be three generations of Dung Beetle within each annual Wildebeest migration.

Another major benefit to migration is the reduction in predation by big cats and hyenas. For the most part, these predators tend to have fixed territories, pride areas or home ranges. Although the migration will pass through these areas, Wildebeest numbers suffer less because these are fixed. This is best explained by looking at Lions, which, with the exception of nomadic individuals, are fixed to a pride area. When the migration passes through a pride area, Lions will feast for a period of 1–2 months. However, after the herds have left the Lions are dependent upon other food sources which also tend to move with the Wildebeest or respond to changes in food and water availability. Consequently, the number of Lions within a pride is restricted

by the amount of game found within the pride area throughout the year. If the Wildebeest were to stay in just one area, the size of the Lion pride would increase. Wildebeest therefore benefit by travelling through numerous smaller prides of Lion on a regular basis rather than staying within the territory of one large pride.

River crossings and other dangers

Animals of both sexes and all ages travel together and can cover long distances in a single day, usually at a slow plodding pace but occasionally in a canter. In the Serengeti, however, they face some major obstacles, such as the Grumeti and Mara Rivers, the scene of some of the most spectacular TV wildlife documentaries! As with the majority of their movements, Wildebeest are motivated to cross the dangerous river by the prospect of fresh green grass on the other side. The sandy banks are very steep in many places and many animals are killed by injuries sustained on the ascent and descent of these obstacles. Once they reach water, the flow of the rivers can be powerful enough to sweep animals downstream where many also perish. At numerous locations along the Mara River, the river is littered with tens, even hundreds, of Wildebeest corpses that are feasted upon by Marabou Storks and various vulture species – nature's garbage-cleaners. These rivers also contain some of the continent's largest Nile Crocodiles, which are ready and waiting for the herd to swim alongside their hidden jaws in the murky waters. Finally, for those that survive these obstacles and make it to the far bank, there is the risk of running into an ambush by Lions that have been watching them in anticipation for hours.

Wildebeest undertaking a treacherous river crossing. Plains Zebra will often wait for Wildebeest to cross first.

Map of the 'Greater Serengeti area'

showing locations mentioned in the text

Lake Victoria

Ruwana

Ndabaka Plain

Western Corrid

3

Ndabaka Gate

D
P

Speke Gulf

Duma

Mwanza

Maswa

Kilometres

| 0 | 20 | 40 |

| 0 | 10 | 20 | 30 |

Miles

Key wildlife watching locations

1 Ngorongoro Crater

2 Seronera Valley

3 The Western Corridor

4 Olmoti and Empakaai Craters

5 Moru Kopjes

6 Ndutu Plains

7 Olduvai Gorge

8 Angata Kiti and Gol Mountains

9 Grumeti River

10 Lobo Valley

Key to the map

River		Park boundary	
Stream		Park gate	
Main road			
Track			

MASAI MARA
GAME RESERVE

KENYA

TANZANIA

N

Mara

Bolongonja

ONGO
ROLLED
REA

RUMETI
NTROLLED
AREA

Bolongonja Gate

Lake
Natron

9 *Grumeti*   **10**

Grumeti

Togoro Plain

LOLIONDO
CONTROLLED AREA

Koma Gate

Orangi

lusabi Plain

Nyabogati

Mbalageti

ldoha
Plain

2

Seronera

Barafu
Kopjes

Ngare Nanyuki

Simba
Kopjes

8

Moru Kopjes **5**

Gol Kopjes

NGORONGORO
CONSERVATION
AREA

Naabi Hill Gate

Serengeti Plain

7

Lake
Ndutu

4

Olduvai
Gorge

Ngorongoro
Crater

6

*Lake
Magadi*

1

MASWA
E RESERVE

Karatu

Lake Eyasi

*Lake
Manyara*

Where to watch wildlife in the Serengeti and Ngorongoro Conservation Area (NCA)

Mammals are particularly mobile creatures, especially those that migrate across national borders, but that does not mean we cannot give you a helping hand by suggesting some of the most productive areas to find them. So here are our 'Top 10' sites to search for the animals you want to see. The really good news is that even if there are few animals around, these are truly beautiful places to photograph and soak up the atmosphere. The site numbers are shown on the main map on *page 18*.

1. Ngorongoro Crater

Needing little by way of introduction, the largest intact caldera in the world contains many thousands of resident mammals in a relatively small area, including the 'Big Five', all of which can be seen on a single game-drive. You could follow the crowd but finding your own savanna animals in the crater is relatively easy and much more rewarding. Vervet Monkeys (*page 124*) and Leopard (*page 28*) can be found in the relative coolness of Lerai Forest on the crater floor and on the forested slopes.

2. Seronera Valley

If the Serengeti has a hub then the Seronera area is it; it is centrally placed and provides great access to the rest of the reserve. It has many permanent pools of water that are home to Hippopotamus and which are used by a wide variety of game including large herds of Cape Buffalo (*page 70*) and African Elephant (*page 62*) that thrive in the surrounding woodland. This is a reliable area to find the big carnivores and several smaller predators also occur, including Bat-eared Fox (*page 58*), which lends its Maasai name *esiro* to the valley.

Ngorongoro Crater and Lake Magadi

3. The Western Corridor
It is a long drive from central Seronera to the Ndabaka Gate at the western end of the reserve but this area is less frequently visited by 'the masses' and can turn up some very interesting sightings, including Patas Monkey (*page 120*) that thrives in the Whistling Thorn scrub here. This area is thoroughly burnt most years and the fresh green shoots that spring up are a great attraction to many gazelle and other antelope and which, in turn, attract good numbers of Leopard (*page 28*).

4. Olmoti and Empakaai Craters
To the north of Ngorongoro Crater lie two lesser-known calderas that are popular with enthusiasts of walking safaris. Access is limited to these heavily forested craters and many visitors have them all to themselves on any given day. There are numerous game species present, such as Eland (*page 84*) and Defassa Waterbuck (*page 95*), and flamingos are often present in impressive flocks on the lakes.

5. Moru Kopjes
This wild area is dominated by huge monolithic domes and situated in the south of the reserve. Many guides consider it among the most beautiful of all areas in the Serengeti. It has traditionally been one of the favoured sites of Black Rhinoceros (*page 67*) but this species is far from a guaranteed sighting here. It is a fantastic area to visit in May and June when the huge migrating herds of Wildebeest (*page 104*) and Zebra (*page 76*) move north-west towards their rutting grounds. From a cultural perspective, the Gong Rock (possibly the oldest musical instrument in the world) and a series of Maasai rock paintings can also be visited.

6. Ndutu Plains
Famous for being the birthplace of the majority of Serengeti Wildebeest (*page 104*), the Ndutu Plains are also home to large numbers of carnivores (both resident and seasonal migrants), including one of the healthiest populations of Cheetah (*page 32*) in Africa. Wild Dogs (*page 59*) are also making a comeback here and a wide variety of herbivores can be found, especially when Wildebeest are present in good numbers.

7. Olduvai Gorge

Often referred to as the 'cradle of mankind,' Olduvai Gorge (which is a corruption of Oldupai) lies on the western edge of the NCA. It is famous for being the site of Mary and Louis Leakey's archaeological dig that unearthed remains and stone tools belonging to *Homo habilis*, one of our earliest known ancestors that lived there around 1·9 million years ago. In addition to its paleoanthropological wonders, this is a great site to watch Red-headed Agama Lizards (*page 140*) and the tracks to the site can hold good numbers of gazelle.

8. Angata Kiti and the Gol Mountains

Rising starkly out of the surrounding flat plains, the huge Gol Mountains are a fabulous spectacle at any time of year. Situated in the northern tip of the NCA, they are home to Klipspringer (*page 91*), Rock Hyrax (*page 114*) and the occasional Leopard (*page 28*). After rain, the surrounding short grass plains, and those of nearby Angata Kiti, are a lush carpet of green and an open invitation to thousands of herbivores. Large numbers of gazelle maintain a healthy resident population of Cheetah (*page 32*) and recently Wild Dogs (*page 59*) have adopted the area. Many of Tanzania's top guides rate this area among their favourite places to enjoy solitude, exquisite views and walking safaris.

9. Grumeti River

Famous for its extraordinary Wildebeest (*page 104*) crossings in June and July and the enormous Nile Crocodiles (*page 130*) that feed on them, the Grumeti is right up there in the amazing stakes! The upper reaches of the river are more open than the well-wooded lower section but the whole area is populated by resident plains game and good numbers of Spotted Hyena, while the three big cats are frequently seen here. African Elephants (*page 62*) and Hippopotamus (*page 68*) are abundant and this is the best place in the Serengeti to find the elegant Guereza Colobus monkey (*page 118*).

10. Lobo Valley

Another great location in the northern Serengeti, the Lobo Valley and surrounding hills are populated with good numbers of Lion (*page 24*), including some of the largest prides in the Serengeti, and Leopards (*page 28*) are fairly reliable here especially around the Lobo Springs. Klipspringers (*page 91*) thrive on the kopjes and the Great Migration of Wildebeest (*page 104*) and Plains Zebra (*page 76*) passes through the area twice a year, heading northwards between June and August and southwards in October and November.

Olduvai Gorge

Mammals

Lion *Panthera leo*

Size: HBT 350 cm / 138" (male), 275 cm / 108" (female); SH 120 cm / 48" (male), 100 cm / 39" (female).

Gestation: 15 weeks.

Recognition: a large, sandy-coloured cat whose tail ends in a hairy tuft. Adult males are significantly larger than females and exhibit the bushy mane for which the species is famous.

Habits: typically active during the cooler hours, especially at night, and tends to spend much of the day sleeping and grooming. However, hunting during the middle of the day is not uncommon, especially when food is abundant such as during the Wildebeest migration.

Where to find: savanna and open plains, rarely forest.

Feeds on: a variety of herbivores ranging in size from hares and young gazelle to Cape Buffalo and Maasai Giraffe. In the Serengeti, Wildebeest and Plains Zebra are most frequently taken.

Among the most popular of all animals likely to be encountered in the Serengeti, the Lion is easy to identify. But it is the behaviour of this creature that is most fascinating and our understanding of it continues to increase with new studies and observations. Most importantly, this is the most sociable of all African cats, living in prides of related females (often 3–6) and their offspring that are dominated by an unrelated male, or collective of males (usually brothers or father-son groups) known as a coalition. Some prides may number as many as 40 animals though this is rare. When numbers reach a high level the pride usually breaks up, particularly when food becomes scarce within their territory, or pride area. The norm is for males to be ejected from the maternal pride when they reach 2–3 years old, which is when their manes start to become visibly bushy. Such males become nomads until they mature, when they then compete with other males for the privilege of heading their own pride. Until that point, males, and occasionally females, will roam across an area without a pride, known as a range. The main reason that all males are forced to move on is to avoid them breeding with related females. It can be a tough life for a young male Lion but, once he has matured and taken over a pride, he can enjoy a wonderful life. He can mate with all pride females and, although he may take the 'Lion's share' on kills, is rarely required to take part in hunting, which is the preserve of the quicker and more agile females. Males will usually dominate a pride for 3–5 years, during which time they may sire many litters of cubs and defend the pride against other males. Typically around the age of ten, and after years of sustained fighting with rival males, he may be defeated by a fitter and stronger male,

Everyone knows that Lions and Spotted Hyena do not get along though once I watched these two enemies feeding together on the floor of the Ngorongoro Crater. The Lioness had caught a fully-grown Wildebeest but struggled to bring down the animal. Suddenly a Spotted Hyena came from behind and started to tear open the rear of the animal and start eating it, at which point the Wildebeest surrendered. The Lioness moved to the rear of the animal and started eating the torn end so the Hyena moved to the front and they continued to feed together.

Mudy

The Lion, the 'King of the Jungle', is a keystone species, its populations reflecting the general health of the environment. To those with the power, please take care of them.

Male

The Moru kopjes area, which is not very big, holds five different prides of Lion – many of which are expert tree climbers. While guiding one afternoon, we witnessed a nomadic Lioness walking close to the females of the Jiwe Chapati pride. Four of them decided to chase her and there was serious fighting until she was actually killed. To me this was very strange behaviour. I have also noticed that these prides have at least two pride males and not just one.

Patena

or coalition of males, and toppled from the pride. This is often the end of his era as he is unlikely to find another pride to dominate. With his strength and speed diminished and being unlikely to be able to make successful kills alone, he may eventually starve.

Female Lion, or Lioness, are longer-lived, frequently reaching 15 years or more. They are the day-to-day hunters of the pride and will often stalk prey together, although each has her own skills and preferred place in the hunt. Once prey has been located, the Lionesses will encircle it and stalk to within 20 m or so before running at great speed and bringing the prey down. Lion lack stamina and rarely chase prey far, frequently giving up the chase once they are beaten. Their key to success is to get as close to the prey as possible without being noticed – which is probably why most hunts take place at night. Once prey has been brought down

it is quickly strangled with a sustained biting grip to the throat, or a suffocating grip over the mouth and nostrils. Due to the abundance of male coalitions in the Serengeti-Mara ecosystem, it is quite common to encounter them on a self-made kill, often on large and dangerous species such as Hippopotamus. Lion are not above scavenging either and take prey from other predators, given the chance.

It is most common to encounter a pride of Lion sleeping or resting under a shady tree, and these huge felines indulge in restful activities for around 20 hours a day.

An important activity you may encounter is mating, which can occur at any time of year as long as females are actively fertile, or in oestrus. Bouts of mating continue for 5–8 days during which time the 'honeymoon couple' may mate 2–3 times per hour, every hour, leaving no time (or energy!) for other activities such as hunting and eating. Each mating session generally lasts for between

5–10 seconds, so if you want to photograph it you need to be ready with your camera.

Three and a half months later, a litter of 1–4 blind and heavily spotted cubs is born in a well-hidden den, away from the pride. Their eyes open after a week and, at three weeks, the cubs are mobile, curious and very playful – but in danger from predators such as Spotted Hyena, Leopard and eagles. However, the biggest threat to the new generation is from a new male Lion who has taken over the pride. Infanticide among Lion is surprisingly common and, although very disturbing, ensures that the new pride male sires his own offspring. Females losing their cubs in this way will be induced into oestrus again within a few weeks and the cycle starts all over again.

Only about 25% of Lion cubs reach two years of age but those that do are showered with affection by their mothers and warmly received into the pride by other females. Social grooming takes numerous forms, including head rubbing and licking, and there are few sights as magical as a harmonious pride taking time to enjoy life and each other. Other communications include the famous roar which is usually given when night falls as a proclamation of territory. Males are the loudest and can be heard as far as 8 km / 5 miles away, though females also roar. Scent marking is also common, with males urinating on prominent bushes and rocks being a frequent sight.

Although Lion are apex predators (*i.e.* they are at the top of the food chain), their numbers have decreased significantly in Africa over the past 60 years, from an estimated 400,000 in the 1950s to just 20,000 today. Much of their former habitat has been lost to an expanding human population and agricultural development, while many thousands are still killed each year as a result of predator-livestock conflicts, including some within the NCA and the surrounding hinterland.

Female or *Lioness*

Leopard *Panthera pardus*

Size: HBT 275 cm / 108", SH 80 cm / 32"

Gestation: 13–14 weeks.

Recognition: a beautiful large, spotted cat with short legs, a long, white-tipped tail and robust build. Also look out for the very long, white whiskers.

Habits: mostly active at night with best sightings often in early morning and late afternoon. Stalks its prey before carrying it up a tree to devour.

Where to find: open savanna, forest and riverine woodland.

Feeds on: a variety of mammal prey from hares to large herbivores up to the size of adult Wildebeest. It is especially fond of Impala, Warthog and Olive Baboon, and also birds such as Helmeted Guineafowl.

Easily identified from the larger Lion (*page 24*) by its heavily spotted coat and white-tipped tail, the Leopard is more likely to be confused with the slimmer, longer-legged Cheetah (*page 32*).

A Leopard's spots are arranged in circles, or rosettes, creating an incredible camouflage that allows it to stalk its prey to within a few metres before pouncing on the unsuspecting victim and killing it with a stranglehold to the throat. Although adult Eland (*page 84*) and young Giraffe (*page 80*) are sometimes taken, the Leopards of the Serengeti rarely prey upon such large animals, possibly due to their relatively small size compared to Leopards found elsewhere. Leopard are famous for their tree-climbing ability and routinely carry prey, often heavier than themselves, in their powerful jaws up

Chief Stalker
The ability of a Leopard to hide in grass while moving with stealth is second to none. Adults have been seen to walk into short grass only 40 cm / 16" high, disappear for 5 minutes and eventually emerge some 20 m / 65 ft away!

into the higher branches where it is safe to feed without harassment from Lion and Spotted Hyena (*page 42*). These two powerful predators are the biggest dangers facing a Leopard, though Leopards are often aware of their presence and steer well clear. Despite being a favoured prey item, Olive Baboon (*page 126*) also represent a threat and troops will often force a Leopard to leave an area, through noisy and aggressive intimidation. Leopard are usually encountered alone, with the major exception being a mother with her cubs. Males take no part in the rearing of cubs and their mating encounters, usually with more than one female within their home range, are kept brief and highly secretive. The commonly heard vocalization of Leopard is a loud pulsating "*saw-grunt*" usually repeated up to 15 times, sounding like a carpenter sawing wood. Home ranges are routinely marked with urine and favoured trees are used as scratching posts, both offering clues to their presence.

Before giving birth, a female will hide in a dense thicket where the cubs (usually 1–4) are born and kept hidden for around two months. It is during this time that the cubs are most at risk from predation by wandering Spotted Hyena. The cubs will stay with the female for the next two years, sometimes less for male cubs, and it is not unusual for two generations of cubs to be encountered together with their mother.

My best Leopard sighting was near the Lobo area in the Serengeti. My guests and I were watching a group of Lioness stalking Warthogs, with a herd of Impala nearby. The Lioness caught a Warthog, causing the Impalas to flee straight into the path of a female Leopard, so she had an easy catch. This Impala let out a cry that attracted the Lions and the Leopard quickly lost her meal, escaping up a tree to watch the Lions eating her meal.
After 30 minutes, the Lions had a break and the Leopard came down and stole the Warthog, dragging it back up the tree out of the Lions' reach. **Patita**

I was taught to identify individual Leopards by their whisker spots and I've used this technique to monitor the extent of their territories. I once encountered a Giraffe that had died of natural causes and saw a male Leopard I knew by the name of Knut feeding on it, and later found another wandering male feeding on the same carcass. For three days, these two male Leopards shared the same carcass, one after another, which made me believe that Leopards are not 100% territorial.
Mudy

This Bohor Reedbuck, weighing almost twice that of the Leopard, was hauled up this tree for safety.

Cheetah *Acinonyx jubatus*

Swa: **Duma** Maa: **Olowuru kerri**

Size: HBT 240 cm/95"; SH 85 cm/34"

Gestation: 13–13½ weeks.

Recognition: a large, long-legged and streamlined cat with a small head. Its sandy-coloured head, coat and tail base are heavily spotted, though its underparts are white. The face has prominent black 'tear-lines' running down from the eyes. The long tail has 4–6 bands towards the end and a white tip.

Habits: mostly active in the daytime, when it searches for prey, but males frequently patrol their territory at night.

Where to find: open plains and savanna.

Feeds on: mostly Thomson's Gazelle and hares, although larger prey to the size of Wildebeest, Topi and Zebra are sometimes taken when several animals hunt together.

Although superficially similar to the Leopard (*page 28*), the Cheetah has a truly spotted coat and is far more slender, like a greyhound in structure. It has a well-deserved reputation for being the fastest land animal on the planet, reaching speeds in excess of 112 kph/70 mph, including an impressive 0–100 kph / 0–60 mph burst in three seconds, when chasing prey. Otherwise, the Cheetah is the lightweight of the 'big cats'. Its delicate frame makes it highly susceptible to damage from scavengers and predators, such as Lion (*page 24*) and Spotted Hyena (*page 42*). They are particularly at risk from these more powerful predators when sitting over a kill and will often give up their prey rather than face a potentially damaging encounter. Cheetah detect their prey by sight, which is exceptionally acute. The black 'tear-mark' running down from the corner of the eyes helps to keep

What's in a name?
The Cheetah is the only feline with non-retractable claws and its scientific genus *Acinonyx* translates to 'no-move claw' in Ancient Greek.

sunlight from obscuring their vision. Sometimes this cat will climb onto a high termite mound, or even a vehicle, for an elevated view of the terrain. Once prey has been located, it is stalked to less than 30 m / 100 ft before being chased over a distance of up to 500 m / ⅓ mile. During this time, the large nostrils swell to allow increased air intake and the respiratory system works overtime to circulate oxygen through the body. The long tail is used for steering and balance, especially when chasing the fleet-footed Thomson's Gazelle (*page 100*) that habitually twists and turns during a chase. At the final moment, the prey is usually tripped before being pounced on and a fatal choke-hold applied to the throat. Because the heart is racing so fast, the Cheetah has to allow its body to recuperate before eating, often for as long as 25 minutes. Once it has cooled down it will gorge itself before circling vultures give away its position to dangerous scavengers. Females live and hunt alone within a home range after reaching maturity at around two years old, while males mature earlier at around one year. Males may live and hunt in a coalition and their territory includes the ranges of several females. Both sexes are promiscuous and each litter may include offspring from several males. Most litters are of 3–6 cubs, which are born with their characteristic spots and downy, grey fur which they eventually shed. A high percentage of young cubs are killed by predators but once they reach about

A mother with her well-grown cub.

six months they are generally safe and able to follow their mother on hunts. However, they are not particularly skilled until 15 months or so. At 18 months, the mother leaves the cubs, which then stay together for another six months, refining their hunting and social skills. When they are about two years old, the females of the family desert their siblings to lead a solitary life. One of the biggest problems facing Cheetah is their low genetic variability, which causes problems with health.

In fact, all Cheetah surviving today are the result of an inbreeding event, known as a genetic bottleneck, that is likely to have occurred between 10,000 and 12,000 years ago. The latest DNA research suggests that as few as 7 Cheetah survived at one point, all of which were descended from the same female.

Unlike other big cats, Cheetah purr but cannot roar. They also produce a loud bird-like "chirp" when trying to find each other and may hiss loudly in the face of danger.

Since 2005, we used to see five Cheetah on the Ngorongoro Crater floor: a solitary male, a coalition of two brothers and two separate females. The crater floor is very flat and these Cheetah had to learn how to overcome the problem of their visibility to prey and other predators that steal their prey. We noticed that females tend to hunt Scrub Hares and baby gazelles, small prey that is often found alone. The coalition brothers were also careful to avoid wasting energy on hunts that might be stolen by Lions and Hyenas and would spend long periods scanning for the competition before they approached their prey, mostly female gazelle and sometime baby Wildebeest. One of the brothers would hide while the other popped up to draw the prey's attention away. This Cheetah always made sure that the prey was between himself and his hiding brother and slowly pushed the prey closer for the kill by his hiding brother. Hunting this way was very successful and they were rarely spotted by Hyenas. Unfortunately, one of the brothers died and the second one, unable to hunt alone, died a few months later. *Mudy*

An energetic youngster takes a break from play.

Serval *Leptailurus serval*

Size: HBT 130 cm / 51"; SH 60 cm / 24"	
Gestation: 9½–11 weeks.	
Recognition: a small, spotted and blotched cat with disproportionately long legs and neck, short tail and large ears.	
Habits: shy, solitary and mostly nocturnal but sometimes encountered in daytime as it hides in long grass, and very rarely with kittens.	
Where to find: open grassland, lightly wooded savanna and open marshes.	
Feeds on: hares, rodents and birds, but sometimes reptiles and amphibians.	

The Serval is a quiet and stealthy hunter that uses its large ears to locate prey in long grass. It frequently pauses to listen for the sound of movement, using its acute sense of hearing to locate its prey before leaping with an enormous pounce. Once caught, the prey may be played with before being swallowed whole. Like the Caracal, this cat is also capable of impressive vertical leaps of 3 m / 10 ft or more, swatting birds clean from the air. These animals prefer to hide from danger, including game-vehicles, and usually press themselves close to the ground to avoid detection.

When threatened, particularly by larger cats, they will arch their back and hiss loudly. Solitary males mark their territories, which usually contain more than one female, by spraying urine onto bushes, while females tend to be accompanied by 1–4 kittens that are well hidden, often in a burrow, long grass or a bushy den.

Given a partially hidden view, look out for the black backs to their ears which show a crisp white spot in the middle.

These two cats may not have the same appeal as their three larger cousins, but anyone fortunate enough to encounter either should consider themselves extremely lucky!

Caracal *Caracal caracal*

Size: HBT 120 cm/47"; SH 45 cm/18"

Gestation: 9–11 weeks.

Recognition: larger than a domestic cat and more athletic in build with a tan coat and delicate black ear tufts.

Habits: solitary and mostly nocturnal but occasionally seen by day.

Where to find: grassy plains with thickets, wooded savanna and rocky hillsides.

Feeds on: birds and mammals up to the size of Impala (*page 96*).

Often called the African Lynx on account of its long-tufted ears, the Caracal is not a lynx at all but a relative of the forest-dwelling Golden Cat *Caracal aurata* of central Africa. Similar in size to the Serval, the coat is tan-red with whitish underparts in adults, while kittens tend to be lightly spotted on their bellies. Despite its size, the Caracal is a formidable hunter that has been known to tackle adult Impala and very large birds, killing them by strangulation. Meetings between rival males can be violent, especially when a female in oestrus is present. Although females may be followed by a male for days, it has been known for them to mate with several males during a single period of oestrus. The litter of 1–3 kittens is typically well hidden but once they are four weeks old the mother will move them almost daily as she travels in search of food.

What's in a name?
The English and scientific name Caracal derives from the Turkish word *karakulak* meaning 'black ear'.

In my 11 years as a guide, I have only had three or four Caracal sightings. They are actually capable of killing rather big prey. What amazes me is that most guests only want to see Leopard, Lion and Cheetah. Maybe there should be more TV programmes about Caracal to share them with everyone! I wish we saw more of these beautiful cats. **Albert**

Wild Cat *Felis sylvestris*

Size: HBT 120 cm / 47"; SH 40 cm / 16"

Gestation: 9 weeks.

Recognition: almost identical to its descendent, the domestic cat.

Habits: solitary, very shy and primarily nocturnal.

Where to find: rocky outcrops, savanna and dry acacia scrub but nowhere common.

Feeds on: birds, lizards and small mammals, especially rodents and hares.

Among the most secretive of all animals to be found in the Serengeti, the Wild Cat is notoriously difficult to find and any encounter with it must be considered very fortunate indeed. Domestic cats are likely to be encountered close to villages and hybridization with the Wild Cat's human-friendly cousins represents the biggest threat to its survival as a pure wild species. A Wild Cat is generally taller and in better condition than a domestic cat and typically shows a lightly striped coat and warm reddish tones behind the ears.

Male cats are quite vocal when attracting mates and pairs come together in season but soon separate. Females rear the litter of up to five kittens alone, usually in an underground den though sometimes among boulders and dense vegetation. Not surprisingly, the Wild Cat "*meows*" and "*purrs*" just like a domestic cat.

Size: HBT 140 cm / 55"; SH 40 cm / 16"
Gestation: 11 weeks.
Recognition: half-way between a cat and a dog in appearance with a heavily striped and blotched coat, banded tail and a distinctive racoon-like face.
Habits: a solitary and nocturnal prowler.
Where to find: well-wooded areas, acacia scrub and savanna, often near water.
Feeds on: just about anything from plant matter and invertebrates to small mammals, reptiles, birds and their eggs (*i.e.* omnivorous).

A close relative of the genets (*page 40*), the African Civet is taller and stockier but, similarly, most likely to be encountered around sunset or at night when it wanders widely in search of a varied menu. Small mammals, such as mice, are leaped upon and seized in the powerful jaws before being thrashed from side to side.

Among the Civet's other impressive attributes is an erectile crest that it raises when threatened, excited or alarmed. During the breeding season, males will serenade potential mates with a laughing "*hahaha*" call. In the daytime, this animal will rest in dense vegetation but only the females make a nest in which up to four pups are reared.

Does this make scents to you?

African Civets mark their territory with a highly pungent scent secreted from the perineal glands at their rear. Unfortunately for the Civet, it was discovered 100s of years ago that this yellow waxy secretion, known as *civetone*, has the ability to fix the scent of flowers in the production of perfumes. Consequently, civets were kept in huge numbers around the world, generally in poor conditions. Thanks to progressive action by animal welfare groups, such as the World Society for the Protection of Animals (WSPA), this cruel practice has all but stopped, with major perfume manufacturers adopting a synthetic substitute since the 1990s.

Small-spotted Genet *Genetta genetta*

Also known as Common Genet

Size: HBT 100 cm / 39"

Gestation: 10–11 weeks.

Recognition: off-white coat colour shows linear black spots, a black stripe down the spine, and an evenly-barred tail usually tipped with white.

Habits: nocturnal and can become tame around camps and lodges.

Where to find: prefers drier habitats and is more frequently seen on the ground than the Large-spotted Genet.

Feeds on: an omnivorous diet of fruits, birds, invertebrates, small mammals and reptiles.

Genet Generalities

Genets are long-tailed, short-legged *viverrids*, a family that also includes the African Civet (*page 39*). Unlike that terrestrial species, both genets featured here are mainly tree-dwellers that climb superbly though also venture to the ground to feed and scent-mark. Like the African Civet, these cat-like mammals have fragrant scent glands at their rear and often make impressive handstands while rubbing the glands against a tree or bush. Generally solitary, genets may gather together where a substantial food source permits non-aggressive interaction between them. Their diet consists mostly of small rodents, though they will feed on birds, small reptiles and invertebrates, depending upon local availability. Prey is typically leapt upon before being dispatched with a killer bite to the neck.

The leafy nest is usually in a tree-hole, where 1–5 kittens are raised. The young do not accompany their mother on hunts until they are several months old and are usually chased away when they are mature at about six months. Most activity occurs from one hour before sunset until the early hours of the morning and your best chance of seeing one is at your camp or lodge where many become habituated to night-time feeding stations. This is when you are most likely to hear their cat-like vocalizations and smell their not-so-pleasant scent!

Large-spotted Genet *Genetta tigrina*

Also known as Blotched Genet

Size: HBT 110 cm / 43"

Gestation: 10–11 weeks.

Recognition: a large, warm-toned genet with irregular rusty blotches and an unevenly barred tail, usually topped and tipped with black.

Habits: nocturnal and can become tame around camps and lodges.

Where to find: forest and mixed woodland; more commonly seen in trees than the Small-spotted Genet.

Feeds on: an omnivorous diet of fruits, birds, invertebrates, small mammals and reptiles.

Small-spotted Genet ▲

Large-spotted Genet ▼

Spotted Hyena *Crocuta crocuta*

Size: HBT 200 cm/79"; SH 90 cm/35"

Gestation: 16–17 weeks.

Recognition: a large, spotted, muscular predator with a sloping back and large, round ears.

Habits: gregarious and primarily nocturnal, hyena enjoy bathing in pools to keep cool.

Where to find: savanna, sometimes open grassland and marshes.

Feeds on: large insects to big game; an effective hunter and scavenger.

The Spotted Hyena suffers from seriously bad public relations and we feel a strong obligation to put the record straight on this formidable hunter and wonderful parent. Often content to scavenge on just about any carcass it encounters, the Spotted Hyena is also a superb athlete capable of chasing and catching a wide variety of game, especially Wildebeest (*page 104*) and Plains Zebra (*page 76*), but also larger prey including Cape Buffalo (*page 70*). Most prey is run down by small groups of Hyena that may chase for 6 km/4 miles or more before wearing out the exhausted animal, which is unceremoniously eaten alive! Where Topi (*page 103*) are numerous, Spotted Hyena patrol through dozing herds until an unsuspecting victim is quickly taken. Amazingly, a single Hyena can devour a Thomson's Gazelle fawn (*page 100*) within 5 minutes and a large pack of hungry Hyena will consume a whole adult Zebra within an hour, bones, teeth, hooves, EVERYTHING! Specialized teeth and incredibly powerful jaws make light work of the largest animal bones from where the highly nutritious marrow is extracted. Strong gastric juices enables digestion of such bony materials within 24 hours, resulting in chalk-white faeces. At the carcass, vultures are tolerated because of the symbiotic relationship they share; Hyena will often follow descending flocks of vulture to a carcass. Their biggest threat comes from Lion (*page 24*) though a pack of Hyena will often prevail unless an adult male Lion is present.

Spotted Hyena society is female-dominated and highly complex in comparison to other carnivores. Females are noticeably larger than males and the alpha-female, or matriarch, rules the clan, which can number over 50 individuals. Rather bizarrely, a female's genitals are almost identical in size and proportion to a male's and the sexes are best separated in the field by the presence of nipples on the female. Courtship and mating occurs throughout the year and can be amusing to watch as males fear females intensely and the act can be a rather delicate procedure.

Two dark-brown, bear-like cubs are born in a communal den that is usually taken over from an Aardvark (*page 61*) or Warthog (*page 74*). These cubs are the largest of any carnivore in relation to the mother's size and are born with their eyes open. The larger of the two tends to bully its weaker sibling and may eventually kill it. Alpha-female offspring inherit dominance over other females but the males will leave the home clan in search of another once mature. Although the alpha-male gets the privilege of mating with more females, he is not permitted to take part in rearing his own offspring.

Who's laughing now? Hyena communication is primarily vocal and the characteristic *"whooo-woop"* is among the most familiar sounds of the African night and is used as a rallying call. Other calls of note include the giggling cackle and the classic laugh, which is used at the carcass to express excitement and sometimes danger. They also whimper, grunt and growl.

Size: HBT 110 cm / 43"; SH 45 cm / 18"

Gestation: 14 weeks.

Recognition: similar to Striped Hyena but less hairy and much smaller, about the size of a jackal (*pages 54–56*). Its pointed ears are pink and its legs and muzzle are slender.

Habits: nocturnal and often solitary, but can be sociable.

Where to find: dry acacia scrub and less frequently on grassy savanna where termite mounds are plentiful.

Feeds on: almost exclusively harvester termites (up to 200,000 per night!), rarely other invertebrates and their larvae.

Although a close relative and similar in appearance to hyenas, the Aardwolf is the sole species in its own subfamily, due to its diet and physiology. Unlike the hyenas, which have a diet of bone and flesh, this mini-hyena is a termite-eating specialist, retrieving thousands of the ant-like insects at each sitting using its long, sticky tongue, very much like a Pangolin (*page 60*) or Aardvark (*page 61*). It has five toes on its front feet, like the *viverrids* (the African Civet (*page 39*) and the genets (*page 40*)), rather than four as in other hyena, and its rear teeth (molars) are relatively fine compared to those of its bigger, bone-breaking cousins. Although preferring to seek out termite mounds alone, they typically live in loose colonies and will move dens every few months in order to seek out new feeding grounds and allow favoured termite colonies to build up in numbers again. Pairs are monogamous and share parental duties. They use their anal glands to lay pungent scent trails – their faeces smell strongly of ammonia, due to the thousands of soldier termites they consume.

Size: HBT 160 cm/63"; SH 75 cm/30"

Gestation: 13 weeks.

Recognition: smaller than Spotted Hyena (*page 42*) with a bushier tail, shaggier mane and longer, greyish coat with dark stripes running vertically from the spine to the legs. The ears are darker than those of the smaller Aardwolf and are long and pointed compared to the stout, round ears of the Spotted Hyena.

Habits: strictly nocturnal; mostly solitary.

Where to find: dry acacia scrub with open areas.

Feeds on: mostly a scavenged diet of carrion but also invertebrates, reptiles and small mammals.

Rarely encountered, apart from in the dry acacia zone, these nocturnal creatures leave their dens after dark and return well before sunrise. The diet consists of less fresh meat than the Spotted Hyena; it rarely hunts large mammals, preferring to scavenge mostly on bones at partially devoured carcasses, but also preys on invertebrates and rodents. Striped Hyena are less sociable than Spotted Hyena but breeding pairs are family-oriented, with both sexes involved in caring for the pups. These are born with stripes, unlike the dark-brown Spotted Hyena pups. Parity between the sexes is probably a result of lower testosterone levels in female Striped Hyena, and the species is less territorial than its larger spotted cousin. Their dens are frequently self-dug although some are gentrified burrows of Aardvark (*page 61*). Den sites can usually be identified by the abundance of bones littering the site. This species is significantly less vocal than Spotted Hyena and their subtle chattering laugh is unlikely to be heard. Instead, it maintains contact using pungent scent glands at the rear, which, like the African Civet (*page 39*) and genets (*page 40*), it smears onto vegetation as markers.

Dwarf Mongoose *Helogale parvula*

Size: HBT 35 cm / 14"

Gestation: 5–6 weeks.

Recognition: the smallest mongoose, with a rusty-brown coat and tail.

Habits: diurnal, terrestrial and gregarious, with family groups usually numbering 10–25.

Where to find: savanna and riverine woodland with numerous termite mounds.

Feeds on: invertebrates and small reptiles.

At first glance, this mini-mongoose could be mistaken for a reddish squirrel but is in fact the smallest carnivore in East Africa. It is highly vocal and will alert its clan to danger with a high-pitched, muffled whistle "*pissoo*" before running at speed into cover. When it is relaxed, you may also hear a gentle piped whistle, while angry confrontations between individuals are usually punctuated with low growls.

This is a highly sociable mongoose that lives in extended family units ruled by a dominant pair, usually the oldest, which have sole mating rights. Other members of the clan will assist in bringing up the litter of pups and subordinate females may also suckle them. All males are ejected from the clan as they reach maturity and join a new clan. Young females usually stay with the clan and await their turn for dominance before gaining breeding rights. This species is only active in the daytime and sleeps in groups, for safety and warmth, within termite mounds and hollow fallen trees.

Banded Mongoose *Mungos mungo*   Swa: **Nkuchiro miraba**   Maa: **Ekisherin sampin**

Size: HBT 70 cm / 28"

Gestation: 9 weeks.

Recognition: a grey-brown mongoose with heavily grizzled fur, long tail and 10–12 obvious dark bands across the back. Appears hunch-backed when running.

Habits: diurnal, terrestrial and gregarious, with family groups usually numbering 15–40.

Where to find: grassland and open savanna.

Feeds on: primarily invertebrates but also enjoys birds' eggs and small reptiles.

By far the most abundant and frequently seen species of mongoose in the Serengeti, the Banded Mongoose is frequently encountered in extended family units, led by a dominant female. While some members of the clan search for food, most of which is dug up from the ground, others will stand erect on lookout duty and alert others to danger with alarm calls specific to threats from land or the air. The biggest threats come from the air, the most dangerous being the Martial Eagle – although it has been known for groups of this mongoose to mob the predator and force it to drop a captured clan member. Twittering calls and grunts are used to maintain contact as the group searches widely for prey during early morning and late afternoon, avoiding the heat of the midday sun. Large and toxic prey items may be rolled around, while eggs and hard-shelled beetles are repeatedly thrown backwards against a rock to crack them or to make access easier. An entire clan will den together, often in a termite mound or disused burrow with multiple entrances to aid ventilation and access. Outsiders are not tolerated and pitched battles occur at territorial boundaries with fatalities quite common. Within the clan, social grooming takes place frequently and is used to build bonds between individuals. The most aggressive behaviour occurs during female oestrus when numerous males squabble for mating rights. Otherwise, Banded Mongoose life is harmonious, with all members of the clan involved in raising the pups.

Slender Mongoose *Herpestes sanguineus*

Swa: **Nguchiro** Maa: **Ekisheren**

Size: HBT 65 cm / 26"

Gestation: 9 weeks.

Recognition: notably slender with short legs, grey-brown coat and a long, black-tipped tail that is almost as long as the body.

Habits: diurnal, rarely strays far from cover and, although usually encountered at ground level, is adept at climbing trees.

Where to find: forest edge, well-wooded savanna and marshes.

Feeds on: just about anything it can find, including fruits and seeds, invertebrates and small vertebrates, including venomous snakes.

Most likely to be encountered in well-wooded areas, this small but very aggressive mongoose is the only one feared by birds, which frequently raise the alarm in their presence. It is fond of birds and their eggs and frequently climbs trees to find its quarry, using specially adapted claws and foot pads. Unlike the larger but otherwise similar Ichneumon Mongoose that drags its tail behind it, this species carries its tail high off the ground when walking or running. Male Slender Mongoose are polygamous and frequently share a home range with several females.

This small animal is very well known by Maasai as being very clever at stealing meat. Something I'll never forget about a Slender Mongoose was the time I took a cattle herd grazing one afternoon. I heard a funny noise coming from somewhere nearby and decided to follow it very quietly – and there was a Slender Mongoose strangling a Dik-dik! **Patena**

Ichneumon Mongoose *Herpestes ichneumon*

Swa: **Nguchiro mkubwa**
Maa: **Ekisherini**

Size: HBT 110 cm / 43"

Gestation: 10 weeks.

Recognition: large and otter-like, with a grizzled grey coat, long black-tipped tail, short black legs and a dark face.

Habits: diurnal and often encountered in pairs or family groups (up to seven).

Where to find: short grasslands, open savanna and the dry acacia zone but rarely far from water and dense scrub.

Feeds on: invertebrates, fruits and eggs but most fond of small vertebrates, especially large snakes including Spitting Cobra (*page 142*).

This is the longest mongoose and is always on the move. It trots with an obvious 'slinking' action that is not dissimilar to an otter, always with its nose low to the ground and tail trailing behind, sometimes with the black tip raised. It is a good digger and swimmer and takes a wide variety of prey including fish. Males typically have several females within their home range, each of which gives birth to 2–4 young. The young can sometimes be seen travelling together like a train, each joined up to the one in front and always led by the mother.

What's in a name?
The English and scientific name *Ichneumon* (pronounced "*ik-new-mon*") derives from the Ancient Greek for '*tracker*', the famed enemy of the dragon in historical literature.

Marsh Mongoose *Atilax paludinosus*

Swa: **Nguchiro ya maji** Maa: **Ekisheren**

Also known as Water Mongoose

Size: HBT 100 cm/39"

Gestation: 9 weeks.

Recognition: a bushy-haired, all-dark mongoose with a thick, tapering tail.

Habits: mostly nocturnal but also active during the cooler hours of day when it may be seen swimming with head raised clear of the water.

Where to find: lives close to water and marshes.

Feeds on: aquatic invertebrates, small vertebrates and sometimes fruits.

This is the most dextrous of all mongoose and handles food items, such as crabs and clams, with the agility of a primate, and will frequently use rocks to break open tough objects. The soft and sensitive padding on the paws helps the animal when searching for prey underwater.

In the daytime it may be encountered following well-used pathways along watercourses and, if alarmed, take to the water, where it could be confused with an otter. Although the coat is dark, it appears to 'shine' when wet.

This species has been recorded performing an unusual hunting behaviour. This involves sitting with its bright-pink anal glands exposed, which contrast against the dark coat, while emitting squeaking calls. These calls attract small birds to investigate, and once they get close the mongoose pounces on them for a quick kill.

■ White-tailed Mongoose *Ichneumia albicauda*   Swa: **Karambago** Maa: **Olpelis**

Size: HBT 120 cm / 47"

Gestation: 8–9 weeks.

Recognition: a large grey mongoose with black legs and a pointed white-tipped tail.

Habits: solitary and nocturnal, emerging before sunset to patrol grassland and scrub.

Where to find: forest edge, wooded savanna and mixed grasslands.

Feeds on: mostly invertebrates but also small mammals, birds, reptiles and amphibians.

This is the largest of all mongoose species in East Africa and probably the most athletic as it searches for food throughout the night covering many kilometres at a steady trot. It shows a distinctive hump-backed appearance and rarely stands erect on its rear legs as do some other mongoose species. Like the Marsh Mongoose, it possesses an impressive anal gland that produces an intoxicating fluid that is sufficiently pungent to keep predators at bay. This same fluid is also used as a territory marker and during any observation of this animal you may see it rub its rear against grass stems and small bushes, laying a trail of scent as it does so.

What's in a name?
As with the Ichneumon Mongoose (*page 49*), the scientific name of this species derives from the same Ancient Greek word *Ichneumon*, meaning 'tracker' while *albicauda* describes the 'white tail'.

Zorilla *Ictonyx striatus*

Swa: **Kicheche** Maa: **Olpelis**

Also known as Striped Polecat

Size: HBT 60 cm / 24"	
Gestation: 5 weeks.	
Recognition: black shiny coat with four long, white stripes running from the head to the tail; resembling a small skunk. The long, bushy tail is whitish and usually the same length as the body.	
Habits: strictly nocturnal and solitary.	
Where to find: savanna and acacia scrub.	
Feeds on: invertebrates, small rodents and young birds.	

This slender little carnivore is the smelliest of all African animals by virtue of the horrendous scent that is produced from its anal gland. This scent causes a burning sensation in the nasal passage of other mammals. While scavenging at a particular carcass, a Zorilla was observed to keep a pride of nine Lion at bay by spraying them with scent. Zorilla is well-known among the Maasai as it shares the short grassland surrounding the Serengeti where sheep and goats are usually grazed. Several Maasai shepherds have testified to their dogs running away from this small, striped mammal at night though few have ever seen it in the daytime, when it prefers to sleep underground, especially under the roots of an established bush. Otherwise, very little is known about this fascinating creature – the skunk of Africa!

What's in a name?
You may notice that Zorilla and White-tailed Mongoose (*page 51*) share the same Maasai name, *Olpelis*, which means 'stinky one'!

Honey Badger *Mellivora capensis* Swa. **Nyegere** Maa: **Enkoward oonaism**

Also known as Ratel in southern Africa

Size: HBT 110 cm / 43"

Gestation: 26–28 weeks.

Recognition: low-slung, broad and flat-bodied, black below and grey above, separated by a white border. Walks with a distinct 'waddle' and runs at a steady trot with tail raised.

Habits: primarily nocturnal, wandering widely in search of food, often in pairs.

Where to find: widespread where thick cover occurs but avoids flooded areas.

Feeds on: plant matter, invertebrates, honey, large reptiles, small mammals and carrion – a true omnivore.

Notorious for their ferocity and fearlessness in the face of danger, Honey Badgers will think little of taking on a pride of Lion (*page 24*), a pack of Spotted Hyena (*page 42*) or a Leopard (*page 28*) if challenged. When attacking people, they aim for the genitalia – so be warned! A Honey Badger's coat is exceptionally loose-fitting, so if a predator bites into it it can easily turn around and bite back with powerful jaws and tear with its bear-like front claws. The canine teeth are surprisingly small for such a large carnivore but the rear teeth (molars) are perfectly built for crushing its varied diet. This animal has a sweet tooth and has forged a fascinating symbiotic relationship with a bird, the Greater Honeyguide, in order to find bees' nests and honey. Once the bird has located an active nest, it will find a Honey Badger, call to it and then lead it to the honey pot. The badger uses its claws to rip open the hive and it and the bird share the spoils. It has been rumoured that bees become 'suffocated' by the pungent scent released from the badger's anal glands, and thus steer well clear! Either way, the Maasai people prefer to hang their beehives from trees.

Black-backed Jackal *Canis mesomelas*

Swa: **Bweha nyukundu** Maa: **Embarie**

Also known as Silver-backed Jackal

Size: HBT 135 cm / 53"; SH 38 cm / 15"	
Gestation: 9 weeks.	
Recognition: fox-like with a black-and-silver saddle and a black-tipped tail.	
Habits: most active at night and cooler periods, sheltering in cover during the daytime heat.	
Where to find: common across savanna with mixed grasslands and scrub.	
Feeds on: just about anything from invertebrates to large snakes, medium-sized mammals and birds. Also a calculating scavenger at the carcass.	

This opportunist is best separated from the Side-striped Jackal by its black-tipped tail. Despite its smaller size and lighter frame, the Black-blacked Jackal is the more proficient hunter, tackling live prey up to the size of Impala (*page 96*), bringing the animal down after a chase with bites to the leg, loin and throat. At the carcass, it annoys larger predators, such as Lion (*page 24*) and Spotted Hyena (*page 42*), with one Jackal distracting while another jumps in to steal a morsel. Black-backed Jackal are much noisier than Side-striped Jackal, making high-pitched yelps in communication with its pack, especially at night and when food has been located. Black-backed Jackal pairs remain together until one of the animals dies or becomes incapacitated. If this happens the remaining jackal is driven from its territory or killed by its rivals. Black-backed Jackal is the most aggressive of the jackal species.

Side-striped Jackal *Canis adustus*

Swa: **Bweha miraba**   Maa: **Embarie**

Size: HBT 125 cm / 49"; SH 40 cm / 16"

Gestation: 8–10 weeks.

Recognition: similar in size to Black-backed Jackal but differs in having a clearly defined white stripe running along the flanks and a more bushy tail that is usually white-tipped.

Habits: most active at night and cooler parts of the day, sheltering in cover during the daytime heat.

Where to find: wooded savanna and open plains, though rarely seen.

Feeds on: an omnivorous diet but less predatory than Black-backed Jackal.

This scarce resident of grassy plains is less frequently encountered than the Black-backed Jackal but is almost certainly overlooked. The white stripe on each flank, usually edged in black, is the best identification feature – but also look out for the normally white-tipped, bushy tail and smaller ears. This species is less willing to chase adult antelope than Black-backed Jackal but will seek out newborns hidden in the grass. It is also less vocal than Black-backed Jackal, often calling a mere "*hoot*" and a stuttered series of yaps.

Day of the Jackal

The social unit of jackals consists of a monogamous pair that mates for life and discourages outsiders by marking the territory with urine and faeces. They den in a disused burrow where the pair typically rears 2–6 pups. Births generally coincide with a glut of food; in the southern Serengeti/NCA this is when the Wildebeest (*page 104*) are calving, but elsewhere coincides with the migration and antelope calving.
Pups become more playful as they mature and although most young leave the territory after one year, some will stay on as 'helpers' to their parents.

Golden Jackal *Canis aureus*

Swa: **Bweha dhahabu** or **Bweha wa mbuga**
Maa: **Embarie**

Size: HBT 145 cm / 57"; SH 45 cm / 18"

Gestation: 9–10 weeks.

Recognition: a large wolf-like jackal with more muscular proportions than the other two jackals. The muzzle is broad and the grizzled coat is variably coloured but lacks the black saddle of Black-backed Jackal (*page 54*) and the tail is fairly uniformly dark.

Habits: active at night but more so during the cooler periods of the day. Often seen moving with a purposeful trot, pausing before leaping onto prey.

Where to find: widespread in small numbers in open areas including short to medium grassland and rocky semi-desert.

Feeds on: an omnivorous diet that includes fruits, invertebrates, birds and scavenged meat, not to mention a fondness for Wildebeest afterbirth!

Unlike the smaller Black-backed (*page 54*) and Side-striped Jackals (*page 55*) that are endemic to Africa, the Golden Jackal almost certainly originated in Asia or the Middle East and today ranges from the plains and semi-deserts of northern Tanzania, across northern Africa, through the deserts of the Middle East and the marshes of India, and reaching as far east as the forests of south-east Asia. This suggests that it is a versatile species that is well able to adapt to a variety of habitats. In East Africa we see numerous behaviours that help to explain why this is the case. The Golden Jackal is a generalist and has a highly omnivorous diet, foraging for plants, fruits and invertebrates, much of with goes unnoticed to the casual observer, and is more frequently seen hunting for small to medium-sized vertebrates, including reptiles, birds, hares and young gazelle.

It is very capable of scavenging like other jackals but where a wide variety of food is readily available, as it is in the Serengeti and NCA, it seems reluctant to do so: studies showing that in this area less than 20% of is diet is scavenged. Another useful survival adaptation is this dog's ability to go without water for long periods, enabling it to inhabit especially dry environments. As a result it has been able successfully to expand its range throughout the arid area of North Africa.

Courting by male Golden Jackals is a long and drawn-out process, but this helps to establish a strong pair bond that lasts for many years. Locally, litters of 2–9 cubs (usually 4–6) are mostly born between November and February and no doubt benefit from a glut in both rain-related insect irruptions and Wildebeest afterbirth – a rich source of minerals. Offspring from preceding years frequently help the dominant breeding pair with pup-sitting duties and food collection, although none are more vigilant or food-bearing than the mother. This is a similar mode of rearing to that of Wild Dogs (*page 59*). Once they leave the area of the den, pups will travel and hunt for small prey with the parents and helpers and this is when larger congregations may be encountered. In the Serengeti, Golden Jackals have an increased likelihood of encountering other large carnivores. Although it tries hard to avoid Lions and, unlike the smaller Black-backed Jackal, does not scavenge directly at their kills, it will scavenge from Hyenas and Wild Dogs and is capable of holding its own against them when in pairs.

Visitors from North America will recognize a significant resemblance between the Golden Jackal and their native Coyote. It may therefore come as little surprise that DNA and skeletal studies, have shown the Coyote to be more closely related to the Golden Jackal than it is to the two other jackals.

Bat-eared Fox *Otocyon megalotis*

Size: HBT 100 cm / 39"; SH 35 cm / 14"

Gestation: 9–10 weeks.

Recognition: shows a grizzled grey-brown coat with black legs and a short pointed muzzle, above which sits a black eye mask and huge ears.

Habits: mostly nocturnal and sleeps for much of the day, emerging from burrows in the cooler hours to forage. Runs for cover when threatened.

Where to find: short-grass plains and scrubland.

Feeds on: invertebrates, especially termites but also small mammals, birds and their eggs.

Those fantastically large ears are designed for locating prey, down to 30 cm / 12" below ground, which the animal digs up with scurried paws. Combined with an acute sense of smell, very little gets past this tenacious little carnivore. Its jaws contain up to 52 teeth, the most of any African carnivore, which are much smaller, relative to body size, than any other canid and are used for crushing its prey. These attractive little foxes enjoy a leisurely life on the plains, often spending hours outside the den just waiting for the air to cool before heading out on hunting missions. It is not uncommon to see them rifling through Zebra and antelope dung, picking out juicy beetles. It is believed that pairs mate for life and raise up to six pups per litter in a disused Aardvark (*page 61*) or Warthog (*page 74*) burrow. This underground den is core to their range though they will dive down one of many other 'bolt-holes' if harassed by a predator or a vehicle.

Wild Dog *Lycaon pictus*

Swa: **Mbwa mwitu**   Maa: **Osuyani**

Size: HBT 153 cm / 60"; SH 75 cm / 30"

Gestation: 10 weeks.

Recognition: a lean, long-legged dog with a black, tan and white blotched coat, huge ears and a bushy, white-tipped tail.

Habits: sociable, most often seen at rest or trotting in pack formation.

Where to find: savanna, acacia scrub and woodland, but very rare.

Feeds on: mostly antelope, especially Kirk's Dik-dik and Impala.

The Wild Dog is the most successful hunter of all large carnivores, with 85% of all hunts resulting in a kill compared to just 30% for Lions. They hunt in packs, spooking herds to identify the weakest individual before chasing it to exhaustion (with a top speed of 64 kph / 40 mph). Their victims are, rather unceremoniously, ripped apart by the pack while larger prey is generally tackled by one Wild Dog grabbing the tail, another the face, while the remaining pack members disembowel the animal. These are otherwise gentle and sociable canids with an admirable social make-up. The pack is controlled by an *alpha* pair, which has the right to breed and scent-mark their range. All other pack members assist in hunting and ensuring the well-being of the litter, which usually consists of 5–12 pups.

All females leave the pack after two years and join other packs, whereas males stay with the pack in which they were born. Injured or older dogs often stay behind with the pups but all are given a healthy share of the kills through regurgitation. Submission and non-aggression are the norm with these dogs, which is thought to help maintain a healthy pack. Their range can extend to over 2,000 km² and animals seen in the nearby Masai Mara are also likely to visit the Serengeti/NCA during their annual movements. Once common in the Serengeti-Mara ecosystem, the Wild Dog was all but exterminated following an outbreak of canine distemper but signs of a comeback are looking positive.

The biggest threat is from herdsmen who kill them in response to livestock losses, so a well-managed education and compensation scheme is required.

Pangolin *Smutsia temminckii*

Also known as Ground Pangolin or Scaly Anteater

Size: HBT 111 cm/44"

Gestation: 19 weeks.

Recognition: has a tiny head and a long body and tail uniquely covered in large plate-like scales.

Habits: Primarily nocturnal but occasionally seen during the day curled up in a tight ball.

Where to find: could be found almost anywhere except in marshes and rivers, but very rare.

Feeds on: ants and termites (*i.e.* it is formicivorous).

This enigmatic creature is high on the wish-list of even the most experienced safari-goer, such is its rarity. The armour of hard scales, made of keratin (just like your fingernails), covers all but the head and underbelly, which it protects by rolling into a tight ball when threatened or sleeping. If harassed by a predator, it will thrash its tail, using the sharp scales to cut like blades. The front claws are long and curved and used for digging into termite mounds and anthills. However, these are cumbersome to walk on, so the animal generally walks only on its hind legs, with the tail used as a counterbalance, and with forelegs raised. It extracts its tiny prey using its very long tongue (50 cm/16") that is loaded with sticky saliva and stored in a cheek pouch. Once common, the Pangolin has been systematically poached across its range for its scales, which are in demand as love charms and by witch-doctors.

This animal is very rare to see and I saw it just once when I was young. When I saw it, I did not know what it was as I had never seen it before. I ran home to tell my father about the funny animal I saw and he decided to accompany me to identify the creature to find it was *Entaboi*. My father said to me that I was lucky and would have a long and enjoyable life.   ***Patena***

Aardvark *Orycteropus afer* Swa. **Muhanga** or **Kukukifuku** Maa. **Enaishir'dani**

Also known as Ant-bear

Size: HBT 220 cm / 87"	
Gestation: 30 weeks.	
Recognition: robust and hunch-backed with short legs, a long pointed snout, big ears and a long, kangaroo-like tail.	
Habits: nocturnal and elusive.	
Where to find: acacia scrub, savanna and open grassland.	
Feeds on: termites and ants (*i.e.* it is formicivorous).	

Despite resembling the South American anteaters the Aardvark is not closely related. It emerges from a self-dug burrow after dark and wanders widely across grasslands using its acute sense of smell to detect active termite mounds. These it tears open with its dagger-like claws, four on the front foot and five on the rear, before extracting as many as 50,000 termites in one sitting using its 30 cm / 12"-long tongue. Aardvark have a light covering of coarse hair over tough skin and are generally grey-brown in colour, but this is often stained by the soil it digs. The heavy tail, white-tipped only in females, can be used as a counterbalance when the animal stands upright – and especially so when males engage in extreme 'boxing matches' not dissimilar to those of kangaroos. Pairs only form briefly during the mating season and the female give birth to a single young. An Aardvark may be evicted from a burrow by another of its kind, or even a pack of Spotted Hyena (*page 42*), and heavy rain has been known to flood them from their holes. Although bad luck for the Aardvark, this could be your best chance of seeing one

What's in a name
The scientific name derives from the Ancient Greek *orykteropous* meaning 'digging-footed' and *afer* 'from Africa'. The English name Aardvark derives from the Afrikaans / Dutch for 'earthpig'

This is a very special animal to see, both for guests and guides. I am amazed at how many holes they can dig in one night as you always see fresh holes all over the place. They are the home providers of the bush – many other animals, especially Warthog, use the holes to live in.   **Albert**

African Elephant *Loxodonta africana*

Swa: **Tembo** or **Ndovu** Maa: **Oltome**

Size: HBT 7·3 m / 24 ft; SH 4 m / 13 ft (although most are smaller).

Gestation: 96–104 weeks.

Recognition: an unmistakable giant with heavily-wrinkled skin, a long, flexible trunk, concave back and huge ears; many have ivory tusks of various lengths.

Habits: active day and night with best sightings often in the morning and late afternoon. Often seeks trees for shade during the heat of the day.

Where to find: almost anywhere including open plains, savanna, forest and wet areas.

Feeds on: a herbivorous diet of grass and foliage and the fruits from a variety of trees.

Needing little introduction, this is the world's largest land mammal and also one of the most intelligent. The sexes are similar in appearance although the larger males have a squared forehead compared to the females' gently rounded head. Their society is based on a matriarchal clan system (*i.e.* it is led by a dominant female) and most large herds encountered consist of related females of various ages and juvenile males. The matriarch is responsible for the well-being of the herd, which relies upon her inherited knowledge to lead them to water and food resources. As the 'boys' become teenagers, they become boisterous and leave the clan, joining up with other males in bachelor herds where they may spend another 5–10 years. During this period they learn the ways of mature males, or bulls, before entering a life of near solitude. There seems to be no set timescale for when a bull enters musth, a period of exceptionally high testosterone levels in his body during which he roams his realm in a lust-fuelled frenzy. He advertises his state with a wet scent that is often seen leaking from his temporal glands, situated between his eyes and ears – and he is easily agitated and often aggressive. A female, or cow, typically becomes fertile once every 3–9 years and advertises her state with low frequency rumbles that can be detected by males from many kilometres away. There is sometimes a fight between competing males, after which the cow will accept the victor by rubbing her body against his.

A herd of females form a defensive shield around their young.

A huge, mature bull.

One of the BIG 5

Each cow experiences a long pregnancy and can choose to postpone delivery for several weeks if environmental conditions are not to her liking. She delivers alone but soon after she has given birth the rest of the herd will approach, make their introductions, and assist the hairy youngster, or calf, to its feet. At birth, the calf stands 1 m / 3 ft tall and weigh around 90 kg / 200 lbs, and suckles from its mother's two teats that are located between her front legs. Later it will suckle from other females within the clan. The bond between mother and calf is exceptional and they are rarely separated, with female calves especially reluctant to stray, even up to the age of nine years. One of the most enjoyable things to watch on safari is a very young Elephant trying to figure out how its trunk works! The trunk is an extension of the nose, contains in excess of 60,000 muscles and acts like a fifth limb. It is a very useful tool, equipped with a prehensile tip with two finger-like projections for grasping. It is also used for drinking, smelling, squirting water, as a vocalization tool and for touching one another. Most Elephants, but not all, have ivory tusks, which are modified upper incisor teeth. These are used for digging up minerals and stripping tree bark, as well as for fighting and defence in males.

An Elephant's rear teeth (molars) are replaced over the course of its lifetime as the previous ones wear thin. Once the sixth and final set of teeth has worn out, the animal can no longer chew food and will eventually die of starvation. The average life-span of an Elephant is about 70 years. The large ears are important as a communication tool and also for heat regulation. On the back of the ears, look out for the extensive network of veins that help to keep the elephant cool when the ears are flapped. There is another impressive network of veins on the soles of its feet. This is vital for communication as the Elephant sends ultrasonic vibrations through its huge padded feet which can be felt by others many miles away. Their front feet have four toes that they use, together with their trunk, to dig up roots; the rear feet have three toes.

When threatened, an Elephant will throw its trunk around, swing its head from side to side and flap its ears vigorously, often followed by loud trumpeting. Should this be ignored, it may make several

An inquisitive one-year-old.

intimidating mock charges before making a full-on charge – although an animal that is startled or suddenly threatened is likely to skip the warnings and simply charge! On average, most Elephants spend 16 hours a day eating approximately 200 kg / 440 lbs of plant material, although in excess of twice that amount has been recorded! Their digestive system is relatively simple and inefficient and as a consequence their dung consists mostly of nutrient-rich plant fibres and is often colonized by fungi. The remainder of the day is spent on the move, relaxing and sleeping. Conservationists often struggle to protect Elephants from farmers and villagers whose crops are destroyed by their actions – but pioneering research into the reaction of Elephants to honey bees may hold the solution to this conflict (see elephantsandbees.com *page 148*). Together with the Wildebeest (*page 104*), Elephants are crucial to the maintenance of the Serengeti-Mara ecosystem, as they consume vast numbers of young trees that would otherwise turn the open plains into a wooded savanna.

In the northern Serengeti, we have good numbers of Elephant, probably because of the mixture of habitats including woodland, river and savanna, so there is a lot of different food available. The best area in Serengeti is around the Seronera valley as there is also permanent water there, good mud pools, and the river is very small with no big crocodiles, so the babies feel safe. I have seen many big herds of Elephants there and they are very relaxed, allowing you to take good pictures. **Albert**

A baby suckling from the teats between its mother's front legs.

One of the BIG 5

The Horn of Africa

Rhino horns are not attached to the skull and are made from keratin, the same protein substance that forms human hair and fingernails. Unfortunately, both Black and White Rhinos are in serious danger of extinction due to demand for their horns from Chinese and Vietnamese pharmacists, who claim the horn has medicinal qualities for fever, rather than an aphrodisiac as is usually claimed. This follows on from the Middle Eastern craze, during the latter half of the last century, of using Black Rhino horn for dagger handles, which caused the population to crash from 70,000 in the 1950s to fewer than 2,500 by 2004. If the high levels of poaching continue, these spectacular mammals may soon disappear completely – so enjoy them while you still can.

Black Rhinoceros *Diceros bicornis*

Size: HBT 4·4 m / 14 ft; SH 1·8 m / 6 ft

Gestation: 65–70 weeks.

Recognition: a huge mammal with a barrel-like physique, short, thick legs and two horns along the top of its head.

Habits: generally reclusive and nocturnal but occasionally bold and shows well in the cooler parts of the day.

Where to find: prefers wooded savanna and woodland, but most likely to be encountered on grassy plains.

Feeds on: a carefully browsed diet of leaves, branches and shoots. Even when feeding in open grassland, it selects herbaceous plants and micro-shrubs rather than grass.

Often the most difficult of the 'Big Five' to see in the Serengeti, the Black Rhino is second only in weight to the African Elephant (*page 62*). The naming of the two African rhinoceros species has been grossly corrupted since their discovery by Dutch colonists hundreds of years ago, with the White Rhino originally being given the Dutch name wijd, meaning 'wide', on account of its long, square-shaped upper lip. The second species was hastily called Black Rhino, no doubt because some individuals appeared much darker – though the colour of the tough skin is usually a direct result of the soil, mud or dust that the animal has rolled in, and little more. The proposed alternative names of Square-lipped (White) and Hook-lipped (Black) Rhino have not been well-received. Separation of the two species is not a problem in the Serengeti as White Rhino does not occur here.

The different lip shapes of the two species can be explained by their different feeding strategies; White is a grazer (*i.e.* it eats grass), and Black is a browser, using its prehensile upper lip to pluck leaves from branches.

Their huge size and horns make them formidable in the face of adversity and they are very rarely killed by Lion (*page 24*) or Spotted Hyena (*page 42*), although very young calves are occasionally taken. Males use their horns to battle, sometimes fatally, over access to females, and the Black Rhino is reputed to have the highest rate of same-species mortal combat of any mammal. Although they have poor eyesight, both their hearing and sense of smell are very acute and it is difficult for any animal to approach them without detection. Any threat is generally met with a loud grunt or sneeze-cough before running away at speeds of up to 50 kph / 30 mph with the tail raised high. Smell is the primary sense used in communication, with adults of both sexes spraying pungent urine onto bushes and defecating in dung piles, or middens, to inform other rhino of their presence. Like Hippopotamus (*page 68*), male Rhino are retromingent, meaning they urinate backwards. Males are generally solitary except when females are in season, when he may follow her for up to two weeks, conducting routine urinalysis (see *The taste test, page 99*). Females are generally accompanied by calves that stay with her until she calves again, and sometimes long after that. Mating is a time-consuming process as males usually make several attempts to mount before success, with copulation then taking up to 30 minutes.

Hippopotamus *Hippopotamus amphibius*

Swa: **Kiboko**   Maa: **Olmakau**

Size:	HBT 4·5 m / 15 ft; SH 1·6 m / 5 ft
Gestation:	34–35 weeks.
Recognition:	a huge pink and grey-brown blubbery giant, with massive front teeth.
Habits:	usually in water during daylight hours, emerging at dusk to graze on land through the night.
Where to find:	major rivers but also seasonal pools, occasionally on land in daytime.
Feeds on:	mostly grass and rank vegetation. Occasionally nibbles on carcass meat.

Pig or Whale?

Great discussion surrounds the origins of the Hippopotamus. As terrestrial even-toed ungulates of the order Artiodactyla, they are classified together with Warthog (*page 74*) and other swine. But many scientists believe they share a common ancestor with cetaceans (*i.e.* whales and dolphins).

Often labelled 'the most dangerous large animal in Africa', the Hippopotamus is often encountered relaxing in rivers and pools where it appears quite the opposite. Most human fatalities are attributed to canoeists cruising on occupied stretches of river or people accidentally coming between a Hippo and its nearest escape route to water. Despite its huge size and short legs, a Hippo will outrun any human and has been clocked at over 48 kph / 30 mph. Those massive front teeth are spear-shaped incisors and recurved canines, comprised of ivory, rather than keratin like the rear teeth (molars). They are used primarily as fighting tools in territorial disputes, often involving intimidation, charging and water-tossing before contact. Hippo are sociable creatures, living in mixed-sex pods dominated by an ill-tempered bull who presides over his stretch of the river and harem of up to 30 females which he defends vigorously. Young males are tolerated within the pod for as long as they show subservience to him, usually by defecating and/or urinating in the face of the 'boss'. This species is well adapted to

An adolescent takes a stroll.

a semi-aquatic life, with its eyes, ears and nostrils placed high on the head, affording it good sensual perception while keeping cool in the water.

During periods of drought, many will suffer from dehydration and burnt skin, though under normal conditions the Hippo is able to sunbathe for about an hour per day. This is thanks to a unique red and acidic skin secretion that offers anti-bacterial and ultraviolet absorption qualities. During these sunbathing sessions it is common to see oxpeckers and other birds de-lousing the Hippo of skin parasites and ticks. Hippo will generally stay submerged for 5–6 minutes but some experienced canoeists claim to have witnessed dive times of up to 15 minutes. Mating takes place in the water, with males lying on top of submerged females, her nostrils occasionally making it to the surface for breath. Birthing of a single calf, rarely twins, usually takes place in the water but sometimes on land close to water. These 30 kg / 66 lb water-babies are able to suckle underwater within minutes. All but the youngest members of the pod vocalize loudly, with numerous grunts and a "*wheeze-honk-honk-honk*" being the most familiar calls. Dominant males proclaim their territory with a painfully whining song, given on average once per month, which sounds like they have a terrible toothache!

At dusk, Hippo commute from the river to their grazing grounds, shuffling along well-worn paths, known as 'hippo trails', which can wear down by several inches. On land, they are less territorial and will graze in mixed pod associations, walking up to 8 km / 5 miles in search of grass, and consuming around 40 kg / 88 lbs per night. They are occasionally seen chewing on a carcass – a sign of nutritional stress rather than enjoyment of a delicacy. Defecation usually takes place in the water during the day and is an interesting spectacle, with vigorous shaking of the paddle-like tail ensuring the muck is spread widely. On land, various members of the pod will shower territory markers, known as middens, with dung. These middens are usually lone bushes that remain well-fertilized for years. Like the Black Rhino (*page 67*), Hippo are retromingent, meaning they urinate backwards.

What's in a name? The common and scientific name *Hippopotamus* derives from the Ancient Greek for 'river horse'.

Cape Buffalo *Syncerus caffer*

Swa: **Nyati** or **Mbogo**   Maa: **Olarro**

Size: HBT 4·2 m / 14 ft; SH 1·7 m / 5½ ft

Gestation: 50 weeks.

Recognition: unmistakable; huge dark cattle with impressive horns and large drooping ears.

Habits: usually encountered in large family herds, or smaller associations of males.

Where to find: swamps, savanna and grasslands, and sometimes in forest.

Feeds on: long grass and rank vegetation.

We have very good numbers of Buffalo in the Serengeti, especially in central Serengeti. When you watch a group of Buffalo, especially a group of bulls, they always walk towards you giving you the 'buffalo look', where they lift up their nose and look at you as they are trying to smell you. They sometimes have very evil-looking eyes and we always say that a Buffalo looks at you as if you owe him money!   ***Albert***

The gregarious Cape Buffalo is often wrongly referred to as Water Buffalo, which is an Asiatic species, and is by far the most abundant member of the 'Big Five' in the Serengeti. It has a reputation for ferocity and has killed many people in Africa over the years – solitary bulls, weighing up to 1,000 kg / 2,200 lbs, being the most dangerous. In large congregations they can be quite timid, even skittish, often stampeding away from a perceived threat, human or otherwise. Lion (*page 24*) is the major predator of Buffalo though calves may also fall prey to Leopard (*page 28*) and Spotted Hyena (*page 42*). An entire herd will form a tight circle around calves and defend them vigorously, whether related or not. Lions prefer to tackle smaller numbers of male Buffalo rather than face the wrath of a herd of females. Buffalo often greet visitors on game-drives with stares, followed by a roundabout turn, head-tossing and a hasty retreat accompanied by grunts and the tail raised high.

A large herd of females, which can be identified by their long, slender horns.

70

One
of the
BIG 5

A male

Ruminants

Ruminants are separated from non-ruminants by their digestive system and, in particular, the presence of four-chambered stomachs. Once plant material has been consumed by a ruminant, it is partially digested in the first stomach, known as the rumen, where bacteria reduce it to a soft mass, known as cud which is later regurgitated and chewed over for a second time. This ensures that coarse plant fibres are processed to maximize the calorific and protein yield for the animal. As well as Cape Buffalo, all the species covered in this book from Maasai Giraffe (*page 80*) to Wildebeest (*page 104*) are ruminants; the other herbivores (Elephant, Rhino, Hippo, Bushpig, Warthog and Zebra) are non-ruminants.

Mature males are very dark-brown to black and often show whitish marks around the eyes. Females tend to be browner, while calves are chestnut-brown for their first few years. A mature bull's horns are fused in the centre, creating a 'boss', making them easily distinguishable from females. The dominant bull is generally the one with the largest horns. Buffalo are prime ruminants (see *above*) and spend much of their day lying down and chewing the cud. Along with African Elephant (*page 62*) and Hippo (*page 68*), they are very good at reducing tall grass for selective grazers and their movements may be loosely tracked by gazelle and other herbivores. Large molars crush the grass that is rasped into the mouth using a thick, prehensile tongue. Buffalo require considerable amounts of water and may spend hours wandering from one source to another during the drier months. This is the period when males break away from the herd to form two types of bachelor group: one for young males aged 3–7 years and another for those aged 11 years and older. The dominant males, aged 8–10 years, generally stay behind to watch over the herd. Younger groups will rejoin the herd upon the onset of rains, while older bulls, unable to compete with the stronger, more virile youngsters may not return at all, preferring to roam together in small numbers – acting like quintessential 'grumpy old men'. Calves are born at the start of the rains and bond closely with their mothers, who are ready for mating with the dominant bull a month or so later.

These males can be identified by their fused horns that create a 'boss', as well as the tangle of hair below their belly.

Bushpig *Potamochoerus larvatus*

Swa: **Nguruwe**   Maa: **Olkupe**

Size: HBT 220 cm/87"; SH 90 cm/35"

Gestation: 17–18 weeks.

Recognition: unlike Warthog (*page 74*), the entire body of this tall pig is covered with a grey, black or reddish-coloured hairy coat; the face and mane have coarse white hair. Runs with the tail held down.

Habits: a sociable hog that gathers in small groups to feed mostly at night but may also be seen early in the morning.

Where to find: requires dense woodland and thickets in which to hide but also ventures to nearby grasslands to feed.

Feeds on: fond of roots and tubers, but also fruits, invertebrates and even carrion.

The Bushpig is a typical hog and has a justified reputation for being aggressive and unpredictable. Generally, sightings are from a vehicle, although Bushpigs can sometimes be encountered close to lodges or camps 'on the hunt' for an easy meal. Most Bushpigs remain 'wild' – choosing to avoid people or dashing to the nearest thicket – but on rare occasions they have been known to charge at a person and attack with their razor-sharp tusks. Bushpigs are highly territorial, and become particularly aggressive to any potential threat when piglets are around. Groups (or sounders) usually consist of a dominant pair and their progeny. However, larger numbers may gather to exploit a particular food source, *e.g.* the fruit displaced by monkeys feeding in trees, when the hogs are quick to devour any fallen fruit, and will chase away other animals (such as Bush Duiker (*page 87*)) that have the same idea. Litters of 4–6 (sometimes up to ten) yellow-and-brown-striped piglets are born during the wet season, coinciding with the greater availability of food. As these pigs love to wallow in mud, it is worth checking suitable places early in the morning.

Warthog *Phacochoerus africanus*

Size: HBT 200 cm / 79"; SH 65 cm / 26"

Gestation: 20–26 weeks.

Recognition: a large-headed dark pig with a shaggy reddish-brown mane, obvious tusks and wart-like growths on the face.

Habits: diurnal, feeds in family groups and runs with the tail raised high – like an antenna.

Where to find: common on open plains and in savanna and forest edge.

Feeds on: grasses, rhizomes, roots and tubers, occasionally carrion.

The fabulous Warthog is a favourite among safari-goers because it has so much personality. Usually encountered in family groups, they can be tricky to photograph on the plains as they are keen to flee from danger. However, in some camps they enjoy grazing on the lawns and digging up nutrient-rich food items, and have become very tame and approachable. Even where they appear tame, Warthogs

What's in a name? Although the Kiswahili name for Warthog is *Ngiri*, the success of the Disney animation *The Lion King* has resulted in them being known widely as 'Pumba', after the Warthog character in that movie. This is an abbreviation of *mpumbavu*, meaning 'idiot'!

must always be treated with respect, as those formidable tusks are razor-sharp and quite capable of slicing through flesh. Both sets of canine teeth protrude from the mouth; the top tusks are the longest but the lower set much sharper – so be warned! The tusks are frequently used for digging but are also used in hog-to-hog combat and defence against their numerous predators. Adult Warthog are favoured by Lion (*page 24*) and Leopard (*page 28*); the piglets frequently being taken by Cheetah (*page 32*) and sometimes birds of prey. At sight or sound of danger a fleeing Warthog will attempt to escape to a bolt-hole, reversing in at the last moment to face any threat with its tusks. This technique frequently ends happily for the Warthog and occasionally very badly for a Lion. When feeding, Warthogs break up the soil with their pointed snouts, tusks

Kneeling affords better access to short grass.

and feet. You may see them feeding on bended knees, resting on thick-skinned, calloused pads with their front legs tucked underneath. While this is a common sight in the Serengeti and the NCA, Warthogs do not practice this habit everywhere. Although Warthogs are very capable of digging their own holes, they frequently take over abandoned burrows of other animals, such as Aardvark (*page 61*), and seem happy to share their den with birds, such as the Sooty Chat, which may provide early warning of approaching danger. In fact, in good company, Warthog can be very friendly and will sometimes even allow Banded Mongoose (*page 47*) to groom them for ticks and other parasites.

Although Warthog have a long, reddish-brown mane, they are otherwise mostly hairless. As a consequence, they have

difficulty with temperature regulation, but cope with this by huddling close together on cold mornings or wallowing in mud or water during the heat of the day. Wallowing causes discolouration of the skin and as a result the animals acquire the colour of the mud, clay or sand in which they bathe. A group of Warthog is known as a sounder and often consists of several related females, or sows, and their piglets. Males, or boars, tend to be more solitary but commonly follow females that are ready to mate. After two weeks of nursing in a birthing den, piglets will follow their mother on feeding trips. Perhaps surprisingly, hogs (swine in general), are the only hoofed animals that produce litters of multiple young – it is not uncommon to see sows with up to eight piglets in tow – although predation takes a heavy toll.

The facial 'warts' of a Warthog consist of thickened skin and are most obvious in males, which have two pairs: one below the eyes and another above the tusks. These warts appear to afford some protection in combat. The warts of females are much smaller, most animals having just one small pair below the eyes.

Plains Zebra *Equus quagga*

Swa: **Punda milia** Maa: **Oloitiko**

Size: HBT 3 m / 118"; SH 1·4 m / 55"	
Gestation: 52–56 weeks.	
Recognition: an unmistakable striped horse.	
Habits: highly sociable, mixing well with other species. Active day and night and regularly enjoys a dust-bath.	
Where to find: grassland and savanna.	
Feeds on: mostly grasses but also other plants.	

Instantly recognizable from our first alphabet books, the Plains Zebra is a nomadic species in the Serengeti, with many roaming resident herds supplemented by vast numbers of migrants from the Masai Mara and elsewhere.

What's in a name?
The Kiswahili name *Punda milia* literally translates to 'striped donkey'.

Although not as populous within the Serengeti-Mara ecosystem as Wildebeest (*page 104*), Zebra can appear to outnumber their more famous travelling companions at times. This is especially so when they move ahead of the Wildebeest and feast on the long grass as pioneer grazers, paving the way for the short-grass specialists to follow. Adopting a safety-in-numbers defence strategy, Zebra are often found in mixed-species herds, although they are better equipped for survival than many other herbivores with superb eyesight and acute senses of smell and hearing. Herds huddle around their

Disputes can become boisterous.

foals at the first sight or smell of danger and the dominant male, or stallion, is an active chaser of predators including Lion (*page 24*) and Spotted Hyena (*page 42*). Zebra are highly manoeuvrable and are often able to outrun predators – though failing that will send a dangerous rear kick into the face of danger, occasionally making painfully loud contact. Like many other plains game, Zebra live in family units, or harems. These are dominated by a single stallion which serves up to six females, or mares. Multiple harems move together as herds. Zebra society is surprisingly complex, with a distinct

This highly communicative species uses vocalization, body posture and numerous ear-flagging signals to get a message across.
These are a few examples:

Neck outstretched = greeting
Ears forward = frightened
Ears erect = alert or friendly
Ears backward = angry
Snort = tense
Loud bray = danger

hierarchy between the mares and their foals, grooming being used as a method of gaining rank. Males without a harem live in bachelor herds until they are old enough to challenge for one – often an aggressive encounter. Upon winning a harem, the stallion inherits mating rights with all the females. The brown-and-cream foal is active soon after birth, staying close to its mother for several months before bonding within the rest of the harem.

A frequently asked question is "Is the Zebra black with white stripes, or white with black stripes?" Most authorities consider them to be white with black stripes, as the white bellies are not striped. However, some evidence suggests that they are black in the womb and acquire the white stripes and belly just before birth. So, it would seem the jury is still out... Whichever way round, the truth is certainly not black-and-white!

A mother and foal

Another frequently asked question is "What function do the stripes serve?" Numerous explanations have been offered over the years but some of the more credible include:

Camouflage – the Zebra's main predator, the Lion, is colour-blind and hunts mostly at night. Therefore, when it looks through long, vertical grass in search of prey, you can understand how effective this flamboyant camouflage could be.

Dazzle – when a predator chases into a herd of Zebra, it must be difficult to fix focus on an individual while being dazzled by a multitude of stripes heading in different directions. Oddly enough, the collective noun for Zebra is 'a dazzle'!

Heat Regulation – black attracts heat and white reflects it, so perhaps this theory has some merit.

Identity – each Zebra has a unique pattern of stripes, so maybe the 'bar-code' theory is true...

Maasai Giraffe *Giraffa camelopardalis*

Size: Height 5·2 m / 17 ft

Gestation: 60–62 weeks.

Recognition: unmistakable with very long legs and neck and a latticed coat.

Habits: moves slowly in loosely associated groups.

Where to find: open plains, acacia woodland and savanna.

Feeds on: deciduous foliage and twigs, shrubs and fruits by browsing but also eats grass.

Giraffe gather in loose associations of females and their young. Older males tend to be solitary, while younger males gather in bachelor groups. Giraffe are collectively known as a 'tower' when standing, or a 'journey' when on the move. Sexing Giraffe is easy, even when the 'undercarriage' is not in view. Males show flattened, bald-topped horns, while females and young show hairy-tufted horns. These horns, or ossicones, are fused to the skull (unlike antelope) and males often show additional bumps on the head, formed by harmless calcium deposits on their skull. Giraffe exhibit an unusual walking style, known as pacing, where both legs on the same side move together. They gallop with a different style of locomotion, with front and rear legs moving as pairs, enabling them to reach speeds of 60 kph / 37 mph. They generally sleep on their knees and for only four to five hours per day, which is considered low in the animal kingdom. The heart is huge (60 cm / 24" long and weighing 11 kg / 24 lb) and exerts double the pressure of most mammals in order to send blood to the brain. There is a complex system of valves that close when the animal lowers its head, preventing excessive blood pressure damaging the brain.

Drinking can be a delicate procedure.

What's in a name?
The scientific name *camelopardalis* derives from the
Latin for 'camel-leopard' on account of its camel-like
face and leopard-like pattern.

Courtship and reproduction is cautiously slow and begins when the female is in oestrus. The dominant male carries out urinalysis with his tongue and typically grimaces with a lip-curl at the taste (see *The taste test, page 99*). Usually, a single calf is born and the female takes sole responsibility for its upbringing, sometimes sharing the tasks with other mothers at a crèche, or calving pool. Generally silent, Giraffe occasionally grunt and bellow, and females whistle to their young if they stray too far. Otherwise, infrasound communication that is beyond human perception is commonly used.

The beautiful Maasai Giraffe is the national animal of Tanzania and very well protected. When watching Giraffe, you may sometimes observe some strange behaviour when a big bull will mount another bull. You would think he wants to mate, which is confusing, but actually it is called 'mock mating' and occurs when one bull shows his dominance over another. Also, I have never in my life heard a Giraffe make a sound.   **Albert**

This female can be identified by her feathery-tufted horns.

A tall story The question of why a Giraffe has such a long neck has puzzled the greatest minds for centuries. In the 19th Century, Jean-Baptiste Lamarck, an evolutionary theorist, suggested that the long neck was an acquired characteristic from previous generations aiming to reach the highest leaves. Charles Darwin agreed with the notion and developed his own competing browsers theory that supported food competition between browsers as the driving force. This theory remained unchallenged for over 150 years though modern research suggests that Darwin's greatest theory of evolution, natural selection, is predominantly responsible. Male Giraffe with the heaviest heads, supported by longer and stronger necks, have the competitive advantage in 'necking' battles (their only form of combat) and mate with more females. Therefore, the forces of sexual selection are dominant over food competition. Stick your neck out – what's your opinion?

These males can be identified by their flat and bare-topped horns.

Eland *Tragelaphus oryx*

Size: HBT 4·35 m / 14 ft; SH 1·8 m / 6 ft

Gestation: 35–39 weeks.

Recognition: a huge, cattle-like antelope, both sexes bearing large, spiralled horns.

Habits: typically shy and usually trots away from vehicles, most commonly seen in large family herds and smaller same-sex groups.

Where to find: open grasslands, wooded savanna, bushy thickets and acacia scrub.

Feeds on: a browsed diet of herbs and foliage but also grazes.

The largest of all antelope, the Eland is a huge animal comparable in size to oxen, with the largest males exceeding 900 kg / 2,000 lbs in weight. This huge mass hinders the animal when fleeing from danger and they tend to run with a steady trot rather than a dash. Their jumping ability is not affected, however, with well-grown animals able to clear a 3 m / 10 ft fence! Herds of females and juveniles often exceed 100 in number, while bachelor groups are usually much smaller and led by a dominant male that is darker and greyer than his younger subordinates. This bull also shows the most impressive dewlap, a saggy flap of skin that hangs from the throat, and a matted toupee of hair on the crown of its head. Listen out for the clicking of knee joints as these animals walk; this is assumed to be social adverts within their non-territorial assemblages. Maternal herds are frequently visited by males that seek females in oestrus, testing their urine before mating with those in season. Unlike the young of most other antelope that hide for weeks, newborn Eland join the maternal herd within one day and begin to mingle with other youngsters in a crèche straightaway.

A mixed herd of females and calves.

A mature male showing the pendulous dewlap of skin on his neck.

Older males appear greyer in colour and develop a rusty brown toupe and hindneck.

Roan *Hippotragus equinus*

Size: HBT 260 cm / 102"; SH 140 cm / 55"

Gestation: 38–41 weeks.

Recognition: a large fawn-coloured antelope with large scimitar-shaped horns, a stiff mane, black face mask and very long ears.

Habits: a shy and retiring antelope that frequents well-wooded savanna and visits waterholes on a regular basis.

Where to find: possibly extinct in the Serengeti although a strong contender for a re-introduction project.

Feeds on: a grazer of common grasses and may also browse on herbs.

Roan is the fourth largest antelope. At a distance, these large, robust animals could be mistaken for horses, and are even named after a horse's coat colour (roan means white mixed with coloured hair). A close view will reveal a completely different animal with an attractive black-and-white face, long tasselled ears and impressive curved, ringed horns. Found in wooded areas with good grass cover, there was only ever a small population of Roan in the Serengeti. However, it appears they have now disappeared completely, most likely due to poaching. Re-introducing animals to the Serengeti from nearby Ruma National Park in Kenya has been suggested. Where they persist, herds of Roan are made up of a single male with a harem of females and younger animals.

Birthing takes place during the wet season and females will hide their young for several weeks; only introducing them to the herd once they are independently capable of escaping predators. Roan appear to be most abundant in areas where there are few other herbivores and, as a consequence, fewer predators such as Lion, Leopard and Wild Dog.

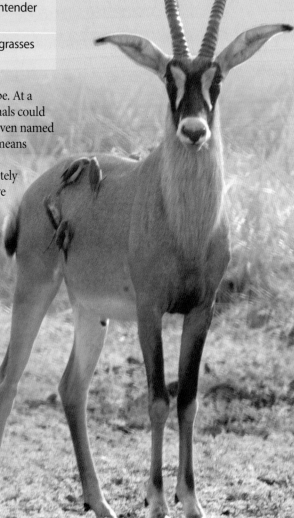

Bush Duiker *Sylvicapra grimmia*

Size: HBT 135 cm/53"; SH 50 cm/20"

Gestation: 18–23 weeks.

Recognition: similar to, but slightly larger than, Kirk's Dik-dik (*page 90*) but separated by the small, black, button-nose, dark blaze running down the snout, and the black-striped tail.

Habits: primarily nocturnal and very shy, usually solitary or in pairs.

Where to find: prefers dense cover in woodland and forest but occasionally seen in the open.

Feeds on: a browsed diet of leaves, shoots and seeds, fallen fruits and sometimes small animals.

This attractive small antelope has adopted the clever habit of following groups of birds and monkeys feeding in fruiting trees, and waiting for fallen fruit to land below. They live in monogamous pairs; the horn-bearing males smaller than the hornless females. Disturbed animals freeze, as does Kirk's Dik-dik (*page 90*), before diving into deep cover. In fact the name 'duiker' comes from the Afrikaans / Dutch word meaning 'diver' on account of this habit. Not surprisingly, these shy creatures hide their young but often raise two offspring per year. Males are highly territorial and frequently scent their trails with dung piles, gland secretions on vegetation, and by scratching trees with their horns.

The black blaze on the snout helps to identify the Bush Duiker from other small antelope.

Steinbuck *Raphicerus campestris*

Also known as Steenbok

Size: HBT 105 cm / 41"; SH 50 cm / 20"

Gestation: 24–25 weeks.

Recognition: a small and thin-legged antelope that is similar to the larger Oribi, but never shows black spots (sub-auricular glands) under the ears or black on the tail. The ears are very large and show fine black markings on the inside. Only males have short, straight horns.

Habits: although a very active feeder at night, it is frequently seen in the cooler periods of the day but is rarely very approachable.

Where to find: lives in savanna and grassy plains but requires a balance of long grass in which to hide and shorter grass in which to feed.

Feeds on: a browsed herbivorous diet of flowers, fruits and herbs but also digs up roots and tubers.

Although fairly common and widely distributed, a sighting of the small Steinbuck is far from guaranteed and should be considered fortunate. Separating it from the Oribi can be a tricky and experience certainly helps – although if a tiny and dainty antelope appears from the grass or scrub and you cannot help but think it has big, silly-looking ears, there is every chance you are indeed watching a Steinbuck. Oribi tend to be seen in small numbers (2–5) and Steinbuck are more frequently seen alone. Pairs stay in 'scent-contact' by laying scent trails using the pre-orbital gland (under the eye) and by defecating in regularly used dung piles. In grassland, they prefer to hide from danger, but if a threat gets too close, it dashes off with a zig-zagging motion; being less inclined to stotting (see *page 92*) than other similar antelope.

Oribi *Ourebia ourebi*

Swa: **Taya** Maa: **Enkaakumuo**

Size: HBT 155 cm / 61"; SH 60 cm / 24"

Gestation: 28 weeks.

Recognition: a slender, tan-coloured antelope with large ears and a clog-shaped head. Both sexes have white eye-rings but only males show narrow, spiky horns.

Habits: avoids the heat of the day but is active early morning and in the evening.

Where to find: uncommon in grasslands and open savanna.

Feeds on: short grass, though often in areas of long grass.

This tan-coloured, white-bellied antelope has an obvious black spot below the ears (the sub-auricular gland), like the Bohor Reedbuck (*page 93*), but is easily told from that species by its smaller size and more slender build. The smaller though similar-looking Steinbuck lacks this black spot. The Oribi is also told from these species by its distinctive black tip to the short, bushy tail, which is flagged-up when running away from predators, in a similar stotting fashion (see *page 92*) to reedbuck. It is when they are threatened that you are likely to hear their main vocalization, a high-pitched, shrill whistle. Like the Bush Duiker (*page 87*), female Oribi give birth in long grass and hide their young for up to two months.

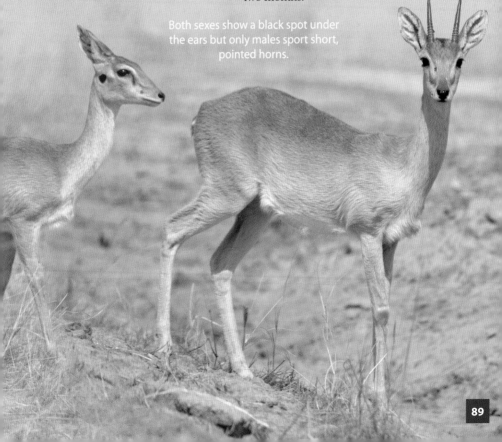

Both sexes show a black spot under the ears but only males sport short, pointed horns.

Kirk's Dik-dik *Madoqua kirkii*

Swa: **Dikidiki** or **Suguya**   Maa: **Eronko**

Size: HBT 80 cm / 31"; SH 40 cm / 16"

Gestation: 26 weeks.

Recognition: a delicate grey-brown antelope with a large nose. Both sexes have a crest of erectile hair between the ears and males show short, spiky horns.

Habits: shy and retiring, will freeze at sight or sound of danger.

Where to find: wooded savanna and riverine woodland; particularly fond of *Croton* thickets.

Feeds on: a variety of leaves and shoots but is a choosy browser.

Although the books say you aways find Dik-dik in pairs, I have seen more than ten animals playing together, marking territories and socialising in the southern Serengeti. In the northern Serengeti we always see them in pairs.   ***Karipoi***

This attractive dwarf antelope is common in the Serengeti and parts of the NCA, and is well known among guides for its monogamous behaviour. Active day and night, if you see one, you can be sure there is another close by. Look out for the classic 'freeze' behaviour, often with a front foot raised. The large, mobile snout is used as a cooling device and is even larger on species of dik-dik found in drier regions. Like the Klipspringer, Kirk's Dik-dik show prominent pre-orbital scenting glands under the eyes that are used to place a sticky secretion on stems as it passes. If you are lucky enough to have Kirk's Dik-dik in the camp you are staying at, also look out for their communal dung heaps that are pawed heavily with scratch marks in the ground.

Note the round pre-orbital gland in front of the eye that is used to lay scent on vegetation.

Klipspringer *Oreotragus oreotragus*

Swa: **Mbuzi mawe**   Maa: **Enkine Oosoito**

Size: HBT 125 cm / 49"; SH 60 cm / 24"

Gestation: 30 weeks.

Recognition: a small, stocky, goat-like antelope with a dark grey-olive coat and short, spiky horns in both sexes. The large, round ears are distinctively patterned on the inside.

Habits: wanders quietly in pairs or small family groups.

Where to find: on rocky outcrops and scree, primarily on the Oloololo Escarpment.

Feeds on: a variety of grasses, herbs and succulent plants.

Meaning 'rock-jumper' in Afrikaans and Dutch, Klipspringer are water independent – able to acquire all the fluids they need from their food. While one animal grazes another will look out for predators, announcing danger with a whistled alarm. Amazingly, they walk on the very tips of their hooves and can balance with all four feet on a rock smaller than the fist of an adult human!

When someone is chosen as a leader (Ologwanani) in a community, their gift from the elders is a Klipspringer blanket made from the skin of about five animals. Once their time as leader is over, they pass the blanket to the next leader.　　*Patita*

The Klipspringer often gives the impression of a small mountain goat.

Mountain Reedbuck *Redunca fulvorufula*   Swa: **Tohe ya milima**   Maa: **Enkakuluo**

Also known as Chanler's Mountain Reedbuck

Size: HBT 162 cm / 64"; SH 75 cm / 30"

Gestation: 32 weeks.

Recognition: darker and greyer above than Bohor Reedbuck with a thicker coat for the cooler conditions at higher altitudes. Females are larger than males, the latter having forward-curving horns.

Habits: most active at dawn and dusk, moving in small herds.

Where to find: well-drained grassy and rocky hillsides.

Feeds on: grasses and herbs.

Unlikely to be encountered away from its preferred habitat of hillside grassland, the Mountain Reedbuck is generally encountered in small groups of 3–7, mostly females overseen by a lone male, or ram.

When they reach maturity, young males are evicted from the group and form separate bachelor groups, though the two types of group may be seen grazing together during the dry season. The bushy tail is dark above and white below, and, as rabbits do, is used as a flagging signal at sight or sound of danger. Like Bohor Reedbuck and Oribi (*page 89*), this species usually shows a black patch under the ears known as the sub-auricular gland although this is not always obvious.

Stotting

When threatened with real danger, both reedbuck species run away at speed, leaping into the air with exaggerated rocking bounces to reveal a flash of white under the tail. This behaviour, which is common amongst antelope species, is known as stotting or pronking, and is used as a signal to predators that the animal is healthy and will be difficult to catch.

Bohor Reedbuck *Redunca redunca*

Swa: **Tohe** or **Forhi** Maa: **Enkakuluo**

Size: HBT 155 cm / 61"; SH 90 cm / 35"	
Gestation: 32 weeks.	
Recognition: a heavily built antelope, tawny-brown above with white underparts. Only males have horns, which are forward-curving.	
Habits: tends to hide in vegetation during the day and feed mostly at night.	
Where to find: most abundant on floodplains, but also in lower densities along narrow river courses with good cover.	
Feeds on: grasses, shoots and reed stems.	

As with many other antelope, the male Bohor Reedbuck enjoys the company of several females within his territory and, in prime habitat, may be accompanied by as many as seven mature females. Both reedbuck species can be separated from other brown antelope by their solid build and large, oval ears. A good view will show the conspicuous dark eyes and nose contrasting with a pale face. Bohor Reedbuck is an abundant species in the Serengeti but can be difficult to observe on account of its habit of lying within long grass in the middle of floodplains. Since this reedbuck prefers to hide from danger, rather than run away, it is sometimes possible to get very close to them on game-drives. (For more information on reedbuck behaviour, see Mountain Reedbuck *opposite*.)

Both sexes show a black spot under the ears but only males sport short forward-curving horns.

Bushbuck *Tragelaphus scriptus*

Swa: **Mbawala** or **Pongo** Maa: **Olpua**

Size: HBT 175 cm / 69"; SH 80 cm / 31"

Gestation: 26–30 weeks.

Recognition: a slim, reddish-brown antelope with a crest on the arched back. Both sexes often have vertical white stripes down the flanks and numerous white markings on the face. Males have straight, spiralled horns.

Habits: usually shy and elusive but can become tame around camps and lodges where it may be seen at any time of day or night.

Where to find: forest edge, well-wooded savanna and riverine woodland.

Feeds on: leaves, herbs, seeds and fruits.

This is a medium-sized, elegant antelope that can be difficult to find where it is not habituated to people. The most obvious sign of its presence is the loud, gruff bark that is used to alert other Bushbucks to a nearby threat, soon after which it often leaps into deep cover with athletic bounds and a white flash of its raised tail. Bushbuck tend to be solitary and non-territorial in nature, staying within a home range that may include many other individuals. However, they may gather in small numbers where resources abound, especially fallen fruits and water. Adults of both sexes are beautifully marked with unique black and white spots and bands on their face, ears, legs and tail; these markings are believed to be used for signalling.

A white-spotted, chestnut coat helps to identify both sexes of Bushbuck.

Defassa Waterbuck *Kobus ellipsiprymnus*

Swa: **Kuru** Maa: **Olmooinko**

Size: HBT 2·8 m / 9 ft; SH 1·4 m / 4½ ft

Gestation: 39–41 weeks.

Recognition: a large, shaggy-looking antelope. Males are dark and show long, curved and heavily-ringed horns, while females are reddish-brown and hornless.

Habits: gregarious, forming large herds of females with young and a few males.

Where to find: common and widespread in open and wooded savanna, often close to water.

Feeds on: mostly grass but sometimes other vegetation.

Waterbuck are not confined to wetlands but do require fresh water for drinking on a regular basis. They prefer medium-length grasslands where they gather in considerable numbers, dominated by a single male that may allow other, subordinate, males to accompany the herd. Otherwise, bachelor herds of young males are found a short distance away from the main herd, frequently engaging in mock-fighting with clashes of horns. It is sometimes claimed that Waterbuck meat is inedible, a myth that stems from the foul-smelling sweat glands under the skin that give the animal's coat a greasy waterproofing. They are less frequently hunted by big cats than other antelopes, possibly because they taste unpleasant. When predators are sighted, Waterbuck will intimidate them by staring and stamping their feet, often giving a loud gruff snort as a warning to others.

The stocky build and long, shaggy coat of the Waterbuck help to separate it from other antelope.

95

Impala *Aepyceros melampus*

Swa: **Swala pala** Maa: **Entarakwet**

Size: HBT 205 cm/81"; SH 90 cm/35"

Gestation: 28 weeks.

Recognition: a slim, elegant antelope with a tan head and upper body, lighter tan layer below and a white belly. There are two vertical narrow black stripes at the rear and the white tail has a black stripe down its length. Only males have the ornate horns.

Habits: most active in the daytime, gathering in large herds.

Where to find: common in wooded savanna and along riverine woodland edge.

Feeds on: very adaptable according to the season. Grazes when grass is green but browses on foliage when grass is brown and dry.

This beautiful antelope is common at the border between woodland and grassland, where it grazes in large herds. Groups of females, or ewes, known collectively as a harem, and their young, or fawns, are dominated by a prime male, or ram. A dominant male controls a harem for up to three months, typically two, during which time he fends off other males and shepherds his flock closely to him. During this period, he chases females aggressively, giving prolonged, barked snorts and all the time smelling their scent with curled-up lips. He has sole mating rights with all females coming into oestrus during his reign, ensuring that the strongest genes are passed down within the herd. Nearby, groups of subordinate and young males watch on in bachelor herds, awaiting the opportunity to topple the dominant

Females can always be indentified by their lack of horns.

male who eventually weakens and shows characteristic black eye patches. (After two months of constant mating, chasing and fighting, this is understandable!) Females can delay birthing for up to a month if grazing conditions are poor. Newborn fawns are hidden from danger in long grass for a week before joining the herd, and young animals gather to form their own crèches, supervised by any female that happens to be nearby.

Impala are a favoured prey item of stalking Leopard (*page 28*), racing Cheetah (*page 32*) and packs of Wild Dog (*page 59*) but are usually too fast for Lion (*page 24*) and Spotted Hyena (*page 42*). When startled, the herd splits dramatically, with animals heading in all directions and leaping with impressive jumps of up to 10 m / 35 ft long and 3 m / 10 ft high in order to confuse the predator. At the same time, they release a scent from glands in their rear shins that enable individuals to relocate the herd once danger has passed.

A resplendent adult male Impala showing the double-curved horns that illustrate his age.

97

Grant's Gazelle *Nanger granti*

Swa: **Swala granti** Maa: **Oloibor siadi**

Size: HBT 190 cm / 75"; SH 90 cm / 35"

Gestation: 28 weeks.

Recognition: beige back separated from white belly with a dark stripe along the flanks. Both sexes have lyre-shaped, ringed horns which are larger in males. Shows a thicker neck and longer legs than Thomson's Gazelle (*page 100*) – the white 'letter-box' above the tail is the best identification feature.

Habits: joins other grazers on the plains after rains but separates during dry periods.

Where to find: open plains and acacia scrub.

Feeds on: grass when green and switches to browsing during dry periods.

This large, elegant gazelle is found in smaller numbers than its diminutive cousin, the Thomson's Gazelle (*page 100*). It is well adapted to dry conditions and while many other antelope travel far for greener pastures, the Grant's will head into the dry acacia belt and browse on shoots and herbage, surviving for long periods without water. Unlike Thomson's Gazelle, the male Grant's does not scent-mark with pre-orbital glands (see *page 90*) but scents using shin glands and dung sites for territory marking. Males defend their patch by intimidation displays, swinging their strong necks from side to side. Females crossing into defended territories are enticed by the male's prancing courtship dance with his nose in the air and tail raised.

From behind, Grant's Gazelle always show a white 'letter-box' just above the tail.

The taste test
Many male animals, from cats to Giraffe, employ a strange habit of testing for whether a female is in oestrus (*i.e.* fertile) by, in most cases, smelling or, in some species such as Giraffe, even tasting her urine. This urinalysis is based on minute pheromone changes which can be identified by the vomeronasal organ located at the top of the mouth. During the analysis, the animal doing the testing grimaces, often with the top lip curled upwards, a reaction known as the Flehman response.

What's in a name?
Both gazelle species were named after Scottish explorers: Grant (1827–1892), who accompanied Speke on his quest for the 'Source of the Nile'; and Thomson (1858–1895), who travelled overland from the Tanzanian coast to Lake Victoria and authored the travelogue *Through Masai Land*.

The stripe along the flanks of a male can range from pale to dark-brown – some individuals with very dark flanks can resemble Thomson's Gazelle.

Females show thin, delicate horns compared to those of the male.

Thomson's Gazelle *Eudorcas thomsonii* Swa: **Swala tomi** Maa: **Enkolii** or **Enkoperai**

Size: HBT 150 cm / 59"; SH 70 cm / 28"

Gestation: 24–25 weeks.

Recognition: dark tan on the back, extending to the tail, and white below, with a bold black stripe along the flanks. Males have slightly curved, ringed horns, while females show two short spikes.

Habits: a communal grazer that mixes well with other herbivores.

Where to find: short grass plains.

Feeds on: predominantly short grass but may browse herbage when grass is dry.

Widely known as the 'Tommie', this charming small gazelle is common and widespread across short grass plains. Although resident in many areas, large numbers also migrate from the Serengeti into the Masai Mara from July onwards, following mixed herds of Wildebeest (*page 104*) and Plains Zebra (*page 76*).

They benefit from the 'lawnmower-effect' of these larger grazers that reduces the longer grass to greening shoots. Adults keep within eye contact of each other and use tail-wagging as a means of communication. Females move extensively in loose groups, passing through the territories of numerous males as they travel. The dominant males defend their territories from intruding males with rapid charges and sometimes clashes with horns.

Although jackals (*pages 54–56*) and Spotted Hyena (*page 42*) readily take newborn gazelle, the Cheetah (*page 32*) is the adults' major predator. Although slower than Grant's Gazelle (*page 98*), which can usually outrun a Cheetah, the smaller Tommie is capable of high-speed jinks and turns which may sometimes save it. When confronted by the slower Lion (*page 24*) or Spotted Hyena, most gazelle perform stotting and pronking manoeuvres (see *page 92*) to display their fitness and agility.

From behind, Thomson's Gazelle always show rusty brown above the tail, unlike the Grant's Gazelle.

Gazelle birth and threats

Female gazelle leave the herd to give birth, often in tall grass. The afterbirth is eaten immediately and the newborn is licked so the mother's scent is fixed on the fawn. Although the fawn can stand within minutes of birth, the mother leaves it for several hours, reducing the risk of drawing attention to it and returns later to nurse the fawn. Most fawns will remain hidden for several days, sometimes weeks with Grant's Gazelle, before joining up with mother and the rest of the herd.

This calf is just a few hours old.

Both sexes show a distinctive pattern from the side – a white belly below a black stripe, above which is a beige stripe and then the rusty-brown back.

Females have very small horns compared to males.

This is a very numerous antelope in the Serengeti and undertakes a mini-migration around the park, but not to the extent of the Wildebeest. They live mainly on the plains and you can often see them on a huge open plain with not one tree in sight, while other animals need shade. When you look at Thomson's Gazelle when they are resting, you will often find that they are facing in an easterly direction, the predominant wind direction, so that they can get air flow over their nostrils. This is when they perform 'nasal-panting', which cools them down; they have much bigger nostrils than other antelopes of a similar size. *Albert*

101

Coke's Hartebeest *Alcelaphus buselaphus*

Swa: **Kongoni** Maa: **Olkondi**

Size: HBT 2·85 m / 9½ ft; SH 1·5 m / 5 ft

Gestation: 34½ weeks.

Recognition: similar to Topi but the body colour is paler brown with off-white buttocks and rear legs. The distinctive horns curve out before curling back in.

Habits: a scarce and shy antelope often found in small family groups.

Where to find: open and wooded savanna.

Feeds on: a selective grazer on medium-height grass and herbage.

The Hartebeest is a widely distributed African species with many local variations and regional subspecies. The subspecies found in northern Tanzania and southern Kenya, *Alcelaphus buselaphus cokii*, is known as Coke's Hartebeest and named in honour of Colonel Wenman Coke (1828–1907), who collected the first specimen. Hartebeest are often encountered in longer grass than their darker cousin, the Topi, and their behaviour is less energetic. Males will often engage in sniffing and nibbling the neck of a competitor in advance of a territorial challenge. Hartebeest and Topi are structurally very similar, showing strong forequarters and a sloping back to lower hindquarters.

What's in a name?
The name is a corruption of *hert*, the Afrikaans and Dutch word for deer.

Compared to the Topi, Hartebeest always appear very pale on the rear.

Size: HBT 2·72m/9ft; SH 1·25m/4ft

Gestation: 34½ weeks.

Recognition: Smaller and darker than Hartebeest, with a chestnut-tan coat. Shows distinctive dark patches on the upper leg and mustard-coloured patches on the lower leg. The back is strongly angled and the horn shape is unique.

Habits: A sociable antelope often found standing on a termite-mound looking for threats, sleeping with its muzzle touching the ground, or running vigorously.

Where to find: Short to medium length grassland and savanna.

Feeds on: A selective grazer of fresh green shoots and herbage.

The graceful Topi is a socially organized antelope with groups adjusting their behaviour according to the size of the herd. In the Serengeti, where resident groups gather, males establish territories that include a number of mature females and their young. These females take this 'honour' very seriously and will chase off intruding Topi of both sexes.

Groups of bachelor males gather at communal display areas, known as leks, where they establish a rank of dominance involving energetic fighting, usually on bended knee, with victors chasing losers away at speeds of up to 70 kph/43 mph. This speed also enables them to outrun most predators, and Spotted Hyena (*page 42*) prefer to stalk them while they sleep. A dominant male Topi will work hard to see off rivals for the privilege of mating rights to his harem of females. Throughout March and April, he performs elegant prancing and high-stepping dances with his tail raised to court them, and engages in rear-end sniffing at regular intervals. He must get his timing right as females are in oestrus for just one day in the entire year. Around eight months later, usually in October, she gives birth to an energetic youngster that remains by her side for a whole year.

Topi are frequently seen with mud-decorated horns and this may be how they acquired their name (the Kiswahili word for mud is *matope*, pronounced *ma-toe-pay*).

White-bearded Wildebeest *Connochaetes taurinus*   Swa: **Nyumbu** Maa: **Oinkat**

Also known as Gnu

Size: HBT 3·4 m / 11 ft; SH 1·4 m / 4½ ft

Gestation: 35–39 weeks.

Recognition: a stocky antelope with a short, thick neck, spindly legs and smooth, curved horns. The glossy, grey-brown coat is variable in tone and shade but usually shows numerous darker stripes and a black face mask contrasting with an off-white, flowing beard.

Habits: typically found in herds of 100s or 1,000s, it mixes well with Plains Zebra (*page 76*), and wanders constantly in search of fresh pasture and water.

Where to find: open plains of long and short grass, acacia scrub and wooded savanna.

Feeds on: an exclusive diet of grass, with a preference for short grass.

The Wildebeest is a strange-looking creature by anyone's standards, but its lifestyle is so impressive that it attracts hundreds of thousands of visitors to the Serengeti-Mara ecosystem each year. Most tourists visit with high hopes of witnessing the spectacle of large numbers of animals crossing the mighty Grumeti and Mara Rivers. However, even the sight and sound of huge numbers grazing on the open plains is breathtaking. Life for Wildebeest is one of perpetual motion; within minutes of birth they are walking and they barely stop for the rest of their lives. They are driven to wander by the need for fresh green grass and fresh water and are perfectly designed to be nature's lawnmowers. When not walking in convoy, or pausing to look out for danger, the broad muzzle is kept low to the ground where

The Wildebeest migration is a very exiting spectacle to follow and, as Tanzanians, we are very proud that the migration starts every year in our country. Thousands of new babies are born on the short grass plains of southern Serengeti, Ndutu and the NCA. The plains here are full of thousands of Wildebeest, always moving for better grass and following the rain. It is an area where new life begins but also where lots of life is taken; there are many predators, like Cheetah, Lion, Spotted Hyena and Wild Dog, that hunt the newborn calves – but this is just Mother Nature's way of keeping their numbers in balance. As one drives around, the chances are good of seeing a female Wildebeest give birth, and I still find it amazing that the babies can walk and run when just a few minutes old.   **Albert**

it continuously takes large bites of grass. Compared to other grazers, Wildebeest have a wider row of front teeth, or incisors, that rasp everything that enters the bite zone. The effect of one-and-a-half million lawnmowers is enormous and, when combined with the fertilizer (*i.e.* dung and urine) that they return to the ground, it is easy to understand why they have a huge influence in maintaining the landscape of the ecosystem.

The Wildebeest migration begins at birth in the southern Serengeti and Ngorongoro Conservation Area (NCA), usually on the Ndutu Plains in February and early March. The breeding strategy is such that around 85% of all calves are born within a three-week period. This ensures that predators, such as Lion (*page 24*), Leopard (*page 28*), Cheetah (*page 32*) and Spotted Hyena (*page 42*), are overwhelmed by the vast amount of food available. Furthermore, calving starts at dawn and is usually completed by midday, causing a huge glut in numbers that cannot be harvested quickly enough by the carnivores. Within 3 minutes of birth, a calf is on its feet and able to follow

A Wildebeest in the Ngorongoro Crater.

What's in a name?

Wildebeest derive their name from the Afrikaans for 'wild cattle', while Gnu is a Khoi Khoi (Hottentot) name for the animal, stemming from their call "*ga-noo*". The scientific name *Connochaetes* derives from the Ancient Greek for 'beard of white flowing hair'.

its mother. Unlike most other antelope that hide their young in the grass for weeks *i.e.* they are 'hiders'), Wildebeest adopt a 'follower' system, in keeping with their wandering lifestyle. Experienced mothers are more successful in rearing their young than new mothers, which have an unfortunate habit of forgetting their calves and consequently losing them to predation. Mother and calf will remain together for a full year and are able to recognize each others' calls and locate each other within a vast, noisy herd if they become separated.

Due to the inherent mobility of the herds and fluctuations in resource availability, Wildebeest do not hold permanent territories or create pair-bonds. Instead, they indulge in a mating season frenzy, called the rut, when males set up temporary territories on the best patches of ground wherever they happen to arrive in early June. It is at this time, after the long rains, that most animals are at their physical peak. These rutting grounds hold approximately 250,000 grunting and prancing males vying for the attention of over 750,000 females. Each male endeavours to entice the females passing close to him, while also attempting to defend his chosen spot against other males, usually with a threatening lowering of horns. The odds are stacked against young and inexperienced males but this strategy ensures that the fittest and healthiest individuals get to pass on their genes. The best 'honker' usually wins!

As the Wildebeest leave the Serengeti and head for the Masai Mara in July and August, they are usually seen in vast herds, mixed with many Plains Zebra (*page 76*) and Thomson's Gazelle (*page 100*). Both these species benefit from following a large Wildebeest herd as it clears vast swathes of tall grass, opening it up for better grazing – and all benefit from increased vigilance against the predators that await them on the open plains. The population of Wildebeest appears relatively stable over recent years though they have experienced some major lows in the past. In the late 1800s, the viral disease Rinderpest spread through introduced cattle into the Wildebeest herds and reduced their population to around 200,000. Today, Rinderpest has been eliminated but Wildebeest are increasingly threatened by illegal hunting in northern Tanzania, where they are currently being poached at a rate of 20,000 per year.

Just one of many thousands of Wildebeest born during the calving season in February and March.

Cape Hare *Lepus capensis*

Swa: **Sunkura** Maa: **Enkitonjo**

Size: HBT 65 cm / 26"

Gestation: 6 weeks.

Recognition: identified from Scrub Hare by the heavily grizzled grey-brown coat that lacks warm tones.

Habits: nocturnal and rarely seen in the daytime except when flushed from dense grassland.

Where to find: open grasslands and open savanna, avoiding wet floodplains and bushy scrub.

Feeds on: mostly grasses but also shrubs and herbs.

These two hares are very similar in appearance though identification based on habitat preference is fairly reliable. Both show a black-and-white tail, which is flashed as a warning to others when running at speed – although both species prefer to hide from danger rather than run. Their huge, long ears separate them immediately from the similar Springhare and their front legs are only half the length of the rear legs. Unlike the Springhare, these true hares do not dig a burrow but sleep in a grassy hollow, known as a form, during the day.

Scrub Hare *Lepus saxatilis*

Swa: **Sunkura** Maa: **Enkitonjo**

Size: HBT 60 cm / 24"

Gestation: 6 weeks.

Recognition: identified from Cape Hare by the contrasty facial pattern, warm rusty tones, particulary to the back of the neck and, often, a white spot on the forehead.

Habits: mostly nocturnal but frequently seen during the cooler hours of the day, often close to bushy cover.

Where to find: common at the grassland edge, in woody thickets and acacia scrub, even close to Maasai villages.

Feeds on: mostly grasses but also other plants.

Springhare *Pedetes capensis*

Swa: **Kamendegere**   Maa: **Enkipuldiany**

Size: HBT 90 cm / 35"
Gestation: 11 weeks.
Recognition: looks like a small kangaroo with massive hind legs, tiny front legs and a long, bushy, black-tipped tail.
Habits: strictly nocturnal, emerging from sheltered burrows after sunset to feed on grasslands.
Where to find: bushy scrub and open grasslands.
Feeds on: a variety of plant matter including grasses and herbs.

This bizarre nocturnal creature is actually a rodent, not a hare. It looks just like a kangaroo and behaves like one too – being able to jump in excess of 2 m / 6 ft in a bound and to travel very fast when threatened. Springhares have long claws on their very long rear legs that are used for digging and traction, but the front legs are tiny and barely used at all. They are fantastic burrowers and can dig tunnels up to 50 m long (although they are typically much shorter) which they can rapidly block when threatened or disturbed.

The eyes are huge, providing exceptional night vision, and the senses of smell and hearing are acute. The Springhare has one of the lowest reproductive rates among rodents, with just a single young born at a time. It does, however, usually breed twice, and sometimes three times, each year.

☐ Unstriped Ground Squirrel *Xerus rutilus*

Swa: **Kidiri**   Maa: **Karbobo**

Size: HBT 45 cm / 18"

Gestation: 5 weeks.

Recognition: a plain, reddish-brown squirrel with an unmarked, greyish tail.

Habits: diurnal, usually in small groups sharing communal burrows.

Where to find: prefers much drier habitats than the Striped Ground Squirrel, especially in the acacia zone.

Feeds on: a variety of nuts, fruits and seeds, occasionally invertebrates.

Unlike most other squirrels you might be familiar with, ground squirrels live up to their name and rarely venture into trees. Despite their similarity to Red and Grey Squirrels of the temperate north, these rodents are more closely related to the North American ground squirrels, a group that includes chipmunks, marmots and prairie dogs, but African ground squirrels lack the obvious cheek pouches of those animals. The Unstriped Ground Squirrel is non-territorial and it would seem that the benefits from predator surveillance outweigh the disadvantages from competition with other individuals. Litters of up to four young are common and family groups communicate with chitters and squeaks, often standing erect with tails flicking, behaviour that is also used in the male's display routine.

The collective noun for a group of ground squirrels is a 'band'.

Grass Rat *Arvicanthis niloticus*

Also known as Bush Rat or Acacia Rat

Swa: **Panya**   Maa: **Enderoni**

Size: HBT 20–35 cm / 8–14"

Gestation: 18–25 days.

Recognition: a nondescript brown mouse with indistinct dark streaking on the back and pale rings around the eyes.

Habits: diurnal; lives in busy colonies, usually burrowing under an acacia root.

Where to find: common in the dry acacia zone, often close to human habitation.

Feeds on: grasses, leaves, shoots & seeds.

Actually a mouse, rather than a rat, this is probably the most abundant and frequently seen of all small rodents in the Serengeti. As with many other mice, they are short-lived (two years is a fine old age) but produce up to twelve young several times a year in a labyrinth-like burrow system. They are a favoured prey of many small carnivores, reptiles and predatory birds.

Look out for the males' unfeasibly large testicles, which are the largest of all the animals in the Serengeti in relation to body size.

Also known as Four-toed Hedgehog or African Pygmy Hedgehog

Size: HBT 25 cm / 10"	
Gestation: 5 weeks.	
Recognition: upperparts are covered in short, cream-tipped spines and both the underparts and head are white.	
Habits: solitary and nocturnal, hiding from heat during the day.	
Where to find: savanna, acacia scrub and rocky semi-desert.	
Feeds on: mostly invertebrates, including scorpions, but also fruits.	

Unlike the Porcupine, the White-bellied Hedgehog holes-up during dry summer periods, a process known as aestivation. This is thought to be in response to food shortages rather than high temperatures *per se* and usually lasts no longer than two months. Females are fertile throughout the year and give birth to a litter of 4–5 pups, each covered in a fine silky membrane which covers the soft spines and ensures the females are not injured when giving birth. The spines harden within a few days.

This insectivore is vaguely similar to the Crested Porcupine in appearance but is far smaller. Unlike the Porcupine, the very sharp spines, not quills, do not detach upon impact with a predator. Instead, the animal often curls into a ball if severely threatened, making some snorts and whistles of intimidation.

I have seen the Hedgehog around the main lodge of Klein's Camp, Loliondo, but have only seen it this once in or near the reserve. In my village though, we see them very often and I have seen a mother with tiny babies, like white rats with no spines, at the entrance to my cattle boma.   *Patita*

Size: HBT 90 cm / 35"

Gestation: 10 weeks.

Recognition: a large, robust rodent with a thick neck covered in a long grey-haired mane. The upperparts are covered in very long white-tipped black quills.

Habits: a nocturnal wanderer, sleeping in a burrow during the day.

Where to find: forest, savanna and dry scrub.

Feeds on: mostly roots and tubers, but also fruit, invertebrates and rarely carrion.

This is the largest rodent in East Africa and famous for the impressive array of long, detachable quills on its back. Contrary to local legend, the Porcupine cannot 'shoot' these weapons at predators but it is certainly capable of defending itself by charging, in reverse, at Spotted Hyena (*page 42*), Leopard (*page 28*) and Lion (*page 24*). Even humans have fallen victim and been stabbed by annoyed Porcupines! More common is the threat display which starts with a loud hiss-like rattle, produced by hollow quills near the tail, followed by all quills raised into an impressive crest to make the animal appear much bigger than it really is. Emerging from burrows at dusk, these animals travel great distances in search of food, much of which is dug up using long claws. Family groups, consisting of a monogamous pair and their 1–2 offspring, are occasionally encountered at night. Unfortunately, many Porcupine are killed by people as they are considered a pest to crops.

Three species of hyrax can be found in the Serengeti and although none will win any prizes for appearance, they are fascinating to watch and understand in so many ways. Hyrax are the closest living relatives of the Elephant found on land (although recent DNA studies suggest that aquatic manatees and dugongs – collectively known as sea-cows or Sirenians – are actually even more closely related to elephants). In general outward appearance, hyrax look similar to rodents but internally are quite different. They have a multi-chambered stomach, like a ruminant (see *page 72*), in which bacteria break down plant fibre. Like Elephant, male hyrax do not possess a scrotum, their testicles being within a cavity close to the kidneys. Females have a pair of teats close to the armpits and four more in the groin area. Although hyrax have well-developed incisor teeth, these are not used for browsing, as in rodents: the lower four are used like a comb for sociable grooming, while the top two form rudimentary tusks. Food is grasped by the molars at the rear of the mouth and is chewed repeatedly. Hyrax are considered to be one of the earliest forms of mammal and exhibit some primitive features, in particular a poorly developed ability to thermoregulate. This is why groups of Rock and Bush Hyrax huddle together for warmth and bask, like reptiles, before they are able to become mobile. Tree Hyrax sleep during the day and emerge from their cosy tree-holes after dark (when they sometimes terrorise tourists with their blood-curdling screams!), so they must be able to maintain their body temperature somehow – though quite how they achieve this is not yet known.

Rock Hyrax *Procavia capensis*

Swa: **Perere mawe** or **Pimbi mkubwa**
Maa: **Enkijujur**

Size: HBT 60 cm / 24"

Gestation: 28 weeks.

Recognition: very similar to the Bush Hyrax but is generally browner and darker (especially in the face) and lacks the pale eyebrows of that species.

Habits: diurnal and communal, often seen sunbathing in extended family groups.

Where to find: rocky outcrops and cliffs.

Feeds on: mostly grasses and herbs.

Southern Tree Hyrax *Dendrohyrax arboreus*

Swa: **Pimbi Mti** or **Perere**
Maa: **Enkijujur**

Size: HBT 60 cm / 24"

Gestation: 28 weeks.

Recognition: dark grizzled-grey upperparts, with a thicker coat than both Rock and Bush Hyrax, and a dark face with a broad snout and usually a prominent white 'moustache'.

Habits: nocturnal, spending most of its time feeding in trees.

Where to find: lives in forest and woodland but rarely seen in the daytime as it sleeps in tree holes.

Feeds on: mostly leaves, fruits and grasses.

☐ **Bush Hyrax** *Heterohyrax brucei*

Swa: **Perere mawe** or **Pimbi**
Maa: **Enkijujur**

Also known as Yellow-spotted Rock Hyrax

Size: HBT 60 cm / 24"

Gestation: 28 weeks.

Recognition: squat and furry; looks like a guinea pig with long whiskers.

Habits: diurnal and communal, often seen relaxing among trees and rocks.

Where to find: common along forest edge and on rocky outcrops.

Feeds on: mostly leaves, grasses and seeds, but also bark, fruits and insects.

The collective noun for Hyrax is a herd.

■ Greater Galago
Otolemur crassicaudatus

Swa: **Komba ya miombo**
Maa: **Kimaongu**

Size: HBT 85 cm / 33"
Gestation: 18 weeks.
Recognition: cat-sized and thick-furred with a long, bushy tail. Usually grey-brown in colour although all-black individuals sometimes occur.
Habits: strictly nocturnal and occasionally visits night-time feeding stations at camps and lodges.
Where to find: wooded savanna, thick bush and acacia scrub.
Feeds on: fruits, seeds, tree sap/gum, invertebrates and, rarely, small birds and their eggs.

Separated from the Lesser Galago by its large size, the Greater Galago is frequently seen on the ground, when it stands upright and leaps with hands and bushy tail raised. When in trees, it frequently walks along branches but is a very capable jumper. Unlike the Lesser Galago, females of this species may be seen carrying young jockey-style on their backs.

Bushbaby Basics

Like humans, monkeys, and apes, galagos are primates – but theirs is a separate and more ancient family. They are very agile in the trees, jumping from one branch to another with great accuracy thanks to exceptional eyesight. They forage alone but communicate with very loud cries, which is why they are often called 'bushbabies', and have excellent hearing thanks to their large, rotating ears. Scent trails are laid with urine and by using scent glands on their chest. They have excellent grasping ability but cannot move their digits independently like other primates. Galago societies are female-led, with males having smaller territories within the home range of a female collective that often gather to sleep in communal nests or tree-holes.

■ Lesser Galago
Galago senegalensis

Swa: **Komba ndogo**
Maa: **Kimaongu**

Size: HBT 40 cm / 16"

Gestation: 16–17 weeks.

Recognition: smaller than a squirrel, with a short, furry coat, a slender tail and a distinctive face pattern.

Habits: strictly nocturnal and always keeps to the trees, unlike Greater Galago.

Where to find: prefers dry acacia scrub with scattered large trees.

Feeds on: mostly tree sap/gum, fruits, seeds, and small invertebrates.

These gremlin-like mammals are great fun to watch as they jump among the trees at night. They are a favourite prey item of owls and genets – if they can catch them! Females may be seen carrying their young in their mouths and depositing them on a safe branch before feeding.

Guereza Colobus *Colobus guereza*

Swa: **Mbega mweupe**   Maa: **Olkoroi**

Size: HBT 160 cm / 63"

Gestation: 25 weeks.

Recognition: a large black-and-white monkey with a long pendulous tail and a draping mantle of long white hair.

Habits: diurnal and gregarious, mostly active in the middle and upper branches of mature trees.

Where to find: mature forest with secondary growth.

Feeds on: mostly fresh leaves but also seeds, flowers, fruits and small invertebrates.

This beautiful primate spends most of its time in the trees, where it rests, grooms and feeds for much of the day. It may also be seen walking along the ground, especially when fallen fruit is plentiful. However, fresh green leaves are the preferred diet, and individuals eat approximately one third of their body weight in leaves every day. Groups move between trees with huge leaps, and bound along branches like giant squirrels. Family units are based around a harem of up to ten females and young, all dominated by a single male that will mate with any female. Aggression towards other males is usually shown by chasing and vocalizing but rarely results in physical contact. Young are born with pink skin covered in white hair and rarely stray far from their mother. The contact call of the Guereza Colobus is one of the greatest sounds of East Africa: a huge, deep, croaking "*ruurrrr*" that travels for several kilometres.

The flowing white hair of the Guereza help to make it one of Africa's most attractive primates.

Patas Monkey *Erythrocebus patas*

Size: HBT 135 cm/53"

Gestation: 24 weeks.

Recognition: an athletic-looking monkey with long limbs, white underparts and a rusty-brown back. The black eye-mask contrasts with a white nose and cheeks and the crown is rich-chestnut. Mature males develop an impressive white-whiskered moustache.

Habits: a ground-dwelling monkey that is usually encountered in a family troop, consisting of a single male and many females with their offspring.

Where to find: most likely to be encountered in Whistling Thorn-dominated areas of the Western Corridor, such as Ruana Plain, and the riverine forest of northern Serengeti, although has been recorded at Ndutu.

Feeds on: a diet of invertebrates and plant materials, with a fondness for ants, fruits and tree gums (*i.e.* sap).

The Patas Monkey is bigger bodied, but shorter tailed, than the Vervet Monkey (*page 124*) and has been called the 'greyhound' of the monkey world; in more ways than one, it really does live life in the fast lane. The front and hind legs are very long for a monkey and offer a clue to its prowess as the fastest-running monkey on the planet, having been clocked sprinting at 55 kph (34 mph). The species lives a predominantly terrestrial life and spends approximately 85% of its day feeding, grooming and resting on the ground. This presents a risk of falling prey to a variety of ground-dwelling carnivores, including big cats and smaller dogs. Being able to run from danger keeps it out of harm's way most of the time, although any predatory chase invariably ends with the Patas eventually taking refuge in a tree. On the matter of tree-dwelling, Patas Monkeys are quite unusual in that, in an attempt to reduce predation, each adult will sleep in a different tree; most other

A female and an immature, with another youngster suckling.

monkeys sleep together in the same tree or nearby trees. Another anomaly of this odd primate is the tendency for troops to contain only one adult male; most other species have a dominant male and a number of subordinate males in the troop. Young males usually leave the main troop voluntarily, though if a new male tries to access females there is trouble. Males will fight with great ferocity for the privilege of mating rights and will frequently use their long dagger-like canine teeth to inflict serious, sometimes fatal, injuries on each other. Otherwise, the job of the male is quite an simple one, his time mostly being spent looking out for danger, leaving the females to run proceedings within the troop.

The 'speed' theme continues through the Patas' breeding behaviour; female Patas are the only African monkeys able to conceive when they are just two-and-a-half years old, and give birth aged three. For the rest of their lives, females will be pregnant or nursing young, and hence have the highest potential population growth rate of any primate of its size. Why the Patas is not among the most abundant of primates can only be explained by their high mortality rates; life spent on the ground clearly not being without its downsides. It would seem that this funky monkey has truly adopted the 'live fast, die young' philosophy!

A male Patas Monkey showing its remarkably long legs.

Blue Monkey *Cercopithecus mitis*

Also known as Sykes's Monkey or Gentle Monkey

Size: HBT 170 cm/67"

Gestation: 21 weeks.

Recognition: two distinct subspecies occur in the region: *stuhlmanni* is a solid-looking monkey with a mostly grey-olive coat, some light-blue fur on the back and a dark cap; *albogularis* is more lightly built and shows an extensive white throat and a rusty-brown blaze down the back.

Habits: diurnal and gregarious, active in the shady canopy of evergreen trees.

Where to find: The form *stuhlmanni* occurs in the riverine woodland along the Mara River of the northern Serengeti, while *albogularis* occurs in the highland forest of the NCA.

Feeds on: leaves, fruits and flowers, rarely invertebrates.

This sombre-looking primate is most likely to be encountered along the roadside in the highland forests of the Ngorongoro Crater but visitors to the far northern Serengeti may also find it in the riverine woodland there. Like many other small monkeys, they live in family groups of up to 30, all led by a single dominant male, which is much larger than the females. He will not tolerate other males in his territory, even his own offspring. Otherwise, troops are very sociable and spend many hours a day grooming each other. This species has a rich vocabulary with particular calls for specific purposes; this includes a soft "*piaow*" for contact, "*jack*!" for threats, and a deep "*boom*" produced by the dominant male as a territory marker.

The blue-toned back, conspicuous pale brow and dark cap help to identify the northern form of Blue Monkey (*stuhlmanni*).

This is the eastern form of Blue Monkey (*albogularis*), commonly referred to as Sykes's Monkey. It is common in the highland forest of the NCA and unlikely to be seen in the Serengeti.

Seventeen forms of Blue Monkey are recognized across sub-Saharan Africa. Identification of the two forms that occur in the Serengeti-NCA should not pose a problem as both the area and habitat in which they are found are different.

Vervet Monkey *Chlorocebus pygerythrus*

Swa: **Tumbili**   Maa: **Nayo kutuk**

Also known as Savanna Monkey

Size: HBT 135 cm / 53"

Gestation: 23½ weeks.

Recognition: the body colour is olive-grey and the face black surrounded by a white rim. This is an agile monkey with a long tail. Adult males show a distinctive powder-blue scrotum.

Habits: a diurnal monkey, at home in trees and grassland. Moves with a bounding gallop along the ground with tail raised.

Where to find: savanna and riverine woodland.

Feeds on: mostly a vegetarian diet of fruits, leaves, seeds and flowers but also takes invertebrates and the eggs and young of birds.

The Vervet Monkey is a sociable primate, found in troops of up to 60. These gatherings are highly territorial and both sexes defend against unwelcome intruders. Even competing males from within the troop will collaborate to deny access to outsiders. Otherwise, the troop is a harmonious place where eating and grooming takes up most of the day and young monkeys get to play and develop their communication skills. The Vervet has a distinct language of its own, primarily used to alert other members of the troop to predators. If young monkeys make the correct call for 'air' or 'land' threats they are positively reinforced, but get punished if they give the wrong call. The commonly heard danger call, a barked "*ra-owp*", is used to warn of Leopard (*page 28*).

There's no mistaking a male Vervet Monkey.

Monkey business

Grooming is a vital social tool used to cement relationships in both Vervet Monkey and Olive Baboon (*page 126*) troops. Each troop comprises many females and young with fewer males (typically one mature male to every three females). Within a troop there is a complex social hierarchy and just by watching patiently, you should be able to deduce which are the dominant males and females. Females remain with the troop for life, where their dominance is hereditary, but adolescent males are evicted from the troop ensuring they never breed with female relatives.

Olive Baboon *Papio anubis*

Swa: **Nyani**　Maa: **Oyekenyi**

Size: HBT 180 cm / 71"

Gestation: 26 weeks.

Recognition: a large, olive-grey monkey with a long, dog-like muzzle. The eyes are small and set under a heavy eyebrow, and the fairly long tail shows a distinct kink near the base.

Habits: often encountered in large troops either feeding, grooming or just on patrol.

Where to find: quite at home in open grassland, wooded areas and rocky escarpments.

Feeds on: almost anything from bulbs and seeds to invertebrates, sometimes taking birds and mammals up to the size of small antelope.

What's in a name? The scientific name *anubis* derives from the Egyptian god of the same name that was represented by a dog's head, similar to that of the Baboon.

Large troops of Olive Baboon are often encountered on game drives but many vehicles pass them by in search of something more

> **Top tip:** avoid standing under Baboons roosting in trees as they habitually shower intruders with liquid excrement!

'exciting'. However, watching Baboons can be very rewarding, so do stop and enjoy! Firstly, check out the males' canine teeth – at 5 cm / 2½" they are formidable 'weapons' that allow the gangs to wander the plains without harassment. Even Lion (*page 24*) prides will think twice about tackling Baboons. The biggest threat to young Baboons is from the air, where Martial Eagle soar, and a complex vocabulary exists to warn of any threats. Leopard (*page 28*) enjoy eating primates and may attempt to tackle an unsuspecting individual on the edge of the troop and face the wrath of 50 others in hot pursuit.

However, the 'Leopard-bark', a loud "*WA-hooo*", is among the most commonly heard of all Baboon vocalizations.

Also look out for females with pink, swollen rumps (perineal swellings), something that male Baboons get very excited about as it means the females are ready for mating. Even lower ranking males get the chance to mate and often spend more time with younger females, forging a close relationship, or 'consortship', that pays-off when she is ready to mate. If a female isn't receiving as much attention as she needs during this time, she will advertise by 'lip-smacking' and flashing her eyelids at passing males (sound familiar?). There is much fighting between prime troop males, all seeking to control females and food resources, and submission is acknowledged by a 'fear-grin'. Older males are more relaxed and adopt a Godfather-style role with infants – although, as a general rule, Olive Baboons do not engage in cooperative caring of infants. The young usually stick close to their mother at all times, clinging onto her underside when she moves and, after three months, by riding jockey-style on her back. Baboons' ranges cover vast areas and one of the reasons they are so successful is their ability to adapt to a wide range of environments. Foraging for food occupies much of their day, and they consume almost everything they encounter. During periods of drought, Baboons will even resort to digging up nutrient-rich rhizomes. This may be supplemented by catching small mammals, especially young gazelle, although this is primarily a male-dominated behaviour that is passed down the generational line.

Mature male Baboons tend to walk with a swagger of arrogance.

Rufous Sengi *Elephantulus rufescens*   Swa: **Ngombo Panya** or **Isanji** Maa: **Enderoni**
Also known as Rufous Elephant-shrew

Size: HBT 40 cm / 16"; SH 10 cm / 4"

Gestation: 5 weeks.

Recognition: a rat-sized mammal with a long tail and long hind legs, but the front legs are noticeably shorter. It has large, bat-like ears raised on top of the head, large black eyes and a long, prehensile snout.

Habits: it is a busy and active hunter in the morning and late afternoon but sleeps at night.

Where to find: lives on the floor of woodland and forest where it roots among the leaf-litter for its invertebrate prey.

Feeds on: small invertebrates, especially ants and termites, which are caught using its anteater-like tongue.

The sengi acquired its alternative name of elephant-shrew on account of its prehensile and trunk-like long nose and insectivorous diet, like that of the similar-looking shrews. The latest scientific thinking supports the existence of a 'superorder' of mammals, the Afrotheria, that places sengis next to other African oddities such as the hyraxes (*pages 114–115*), Aardvark (*page 61*) and, oddly enough, the Elephant (*page 62*), while the humble shrew remains quite unrelated. This just goes to show that, in nature, appearances can be very deceptive.

Listen out for the Rufous Sengi communicating – this involves an Elvis-like foot-tapping serenade in the leaf-litter to mates and rivals in the area, which can be heard up to 25 m away!

The image shown here is of a Four-toed Sengi *Petrodromus tetradactylus*. However, the Rufous Sengi, the species found within the Serengeti and NCA area, is almost identical in appearance.

Nile Crocodile *Crocodylus niloticus*

Swa: **Mamba** Maa: **Olkinos**

Size: HBT up to 7·9 m / 26 ft

Recognition: a long, heavily scaled reptile with a long tail, broad snout and obvious teeth. Colour may be grey, brown or olive-green with black patches.

Habits: a mostly nocturnal feeder but will attempt to take mammals and fish in daylight.

Where to find: rivers and sometimes large marshes.

Feeds on: insects when very young, moving on to fish and aquatic reptiles, birds and carrion. Large Crocodiles will routinely kill mammals such as Wildebeest and Zebra, and attacks on mature Elephants are well documented.

Crocodiles are easiest to watch when basking on the sides of rivers to regulate their body temperature. This is the best time to admire their armour-plated leathery skin, which is covered by toughened scales (or scutes) down the back and tail.

What's in a name? The scientific name derives from the Ancient Greek *kroko~* meaning pebble and *~deilos* meaning worm; *niloticus* refers to the River Nile.

The many teeth, variable in size and length, are perfect for grasping and tearing apart their food. The ears, eyes and nostrils are set on the top of the head, allowing an animal to be 99% submerged but still able to see, smell and breathe. The Nile Crocodile of the Mara and Grumeti Rivers are among the largest remaining in Africa today and frequently exceed 6 m / 20 ft in length and 1,000 kg / 2,200 lbs in weight, and can live to over 100 years old. This is thanks to the annual abundance of meat when Wildebeest (*page 104*) and Plains Zebra (*page 76*) cross these big rivers during the Great Migration. Many animals are killed by Crocodiles, which drown their prey and keep the corpse underwater to soften it. However, many more animals simply drown in the act of crossing. The same rivers are also home to huge catfish, which Crocodiles herd into the shallows and catch in their powerful jaws. Due to their ectothermic metabolism, Crocodiles can survive for months without food. This is just as well, as the plains game heads elsewhere for 8 months of the year. Crocodiles will generally stay submerged for just a few minutes but if they choose to sleep underwater, they can reduce their heart rate and remain there for two hours. Male Crocodiles mature at around the age of 10, by which time they have reached about 3 m / 10 ft in length; females of a similar age are 30% smaller. Mature males become increasingly territorial and court the females in their area. Mating takes place in the water, after which the female searches for a quiet, sandy bank where she lays an average of 50 eggs in a shallow hole. The ambient temperature determines the sex of the young: above 30 °C (86 °F) creates males and below 30 °C females. The adult female fasts for three months while the young develop, watching out for marauding monitor lizards (*page 132*). Upon hearing the high-pitched calls of the young before they hatch, she will return to help dig them out. Like many birds, hatchlings are born with an egg-tooth, which helps them chip their way out of the shell. Once they hatch, the young head straight for the water.

The 30 cm / 12" mini-crocs face a huge test for survival as they are favoured prey of the African Fish Eagle and Yellow-billed Stork. They immediately embark on a predatory lifestyle of their own, catching frogs and insects, and grow an average of 30 cm / 12" a year. Strangely enough, it is widely considered that Crocodiles are more closely related to modern birds than modern lizards, as they share many common features, including a four-chambered heart, rather than a three-chambered heart as in other reptiles.

Top fact: have you ever wondered about the expression 'crocodile tears'? Just like humans, crocodiles possess lachrymal glands that produce real tears. These are not emotionally driven, however, but act like eye-drops to cleanse the eyes.

Savanna Monitor *Varanus albigularis*

Swa: **Kenge** Maa: **Olmaima**

Also known as the Rock Monitor, this is the heaviest lizard in Africa. Although similar to the Nile Monitor, the head is a very different shape, with a bulbous snout and higher forehead. It can swim well but is far less likely to be encountered in the water than the Nile Monitor.

Monitors are strong, muscular lizards with tough leathery skin. A close view reveals many bead-like scales. They are generally sluggish creatures that amble along with their long, forked tongues flicking and 'tasting' the air for food. When threatened or disturbed they run very fast and with a distinct swagger, raising their hefty bodies clear of the ground.

Nile Monitor *Varanus niloticus*

Swa: **Buru kenge** Maa: **Olmaima**

This is the longest lizard in Africa. It is an excellent swimmer and frequently catches fish underwater. Its distinctive writhing, snake-like motion in the water can be a good feature to separate it from small crocodiles. The raised eyes and nostrils are good indicators of the Nile Monitor's aquatic nature.

Trying to catch monitors is very dangerous as they can cut deeply into the skin with their sharp claws, knock grown men over with a hard smack of the tail and bite very hard and painfully despite their blunt teeth. As monitors routinely feed on decaying matter, they often carry the toxic bacterium *Clostridium botulinum* that causes Botulism, a paralysing and often fatal illness. Bizarrely, this is the same toxin used in Botox cosmetic surgery.

Size: HBT 200 cm / 6½ ft

Recognition: variable but most are dark-grey with some light barring on the body and tail, and a pale throat. The head is shorter and broader than that of the Nile Monitor.

Habits: usually encountered on the ground but also climbs trees.

Where to find: open and wooded savanna, especially with termite mounds.

Feeds on: a variety of invertebrates but also small mammals, other reptiles, birds and their eggs.

Size: HBT 250 cm / 8 ft

Recognition: usually dark-grey or olive-green with conspicuous yellow stripes and markings, and a heavily banded tail.

Habits: spends much of the day patrolling for food and runs quickly when threatened.

Where to find: common near water but also found up trees in wooded savanna and in open grassland.

Feeds on: pretty much anything it can catch, including fish, mammals and birds. It has a taste for crocodile and birds' eggs and will readily scavenge at a carcass and root through lodge waste tips.

Leopard Tortoise *Geochelone pardalis*

Swa: **Kobe** Maa: **Oloikuma**

Size: HBT 70 cm / 28"

Recognition: the tall, domed shell, or carapace, has a well-marked black-and-gold pattern.

Habits: walks slowly in search of its next meal during all but the hottest parts of the day.

Where to find: open and wooded savanna.

Feeds on: a strictly vegetarian diet, mostly of grass and thistles.

This is the largest tortoise in Africa and the fourth largest in the world, with the most impressive specimens weighing in at 40 kg / 88 lbs. They are long-lived animals that can reach 100 years old or more in the right conditions. They can retract their armoured head and legs into their shell so have few predators, though Lions will occasionally use them as playthings before tiring and letting them go. Tortoises can move remarkably fast when they choose to and can manoeuvre well over rocky ground. Each shell pattern is as unique as a fingerprint. The male Leopard Tortoise is an aggressive and boisterous lover, grunting noisily and ramming the female's shell to court her, often accompanied by several rival males climbing over the same female. She lays an average of 10 eggs in a hole and these take up to a year to hatch.

What's in a name? The scientific name *pardalis* is the same as the Leopard, meaning panther, on account of the distinctive shell pattern.

Top tip: avoid touching or picking up a tortoise as some are known to carry *Salmonella* bacteria.

134

Helmeted Terrapin *Pelomedusa subrufa*   Swa: **Kasa** Maa: **Oloikuma lankare**

Size: HBT 30 cm / 12"

Recognition: has a flatter, more plain-coloured shell than the Leopard Tortoise, often being matt black or brown. The yellowish head and legs are also longer.

Habits: often seen basking on rocks or branches before dropping into water when disturbed. They wander widely in search of new pools, especially during the rains, and are often seen crossing tracks.

Where to find: seasonally common in marshes and small pools but rarely in large rivers.

Feeds on: almost anything it can catch, including tadpoles, worms and crustaceans but also carrion and plant matter.

Also known as the Marsh Terrapin, legend has it that this reptile literally 'fell from the sky' with the first rains! In actual fact, it simply buries itself in the mud when water becomes scarce, a behaviour known as aestivation. This strategy enables the Terrapin to avoid high temperatures and the risk of drying out by entering a dormant state with a reduced metabolic rate. Male terrapins can be identified by their longer, thicker, pointed tails and are sometimes seen courting females with a nodding head action. Up to 30 eggs are buried by the female and these hatch around three months later.

The shield reptiles (*i.e.* tortoises, turtles and terrapins) belong to a group known as Chelonians, and the Helmeted Terrapin belongs to a sub-order known as Pleurodira, which translates to "side-necked". When threatened, this species is able to withdraw its head into its shell sideways, which enables it to keep one eye on the danger. In addition to its hard shell, it is also able to spray a foul-smelling liquid from glands under the skin and is very likely to scratch and bite if handled.

135

Flap-necked Chameleon *Chamaeleo dilepis*

Swa: **Kinyonga** Maa: **Tanki**

Size: HBT 43 cm / 17"

Recognition: a chunky, hunch-backed lizard of variable colouration, with swivelling eye-sockets and a long and curly prehensile tail.

Habits: typically hides in vegetation but may be found crossing tracks.

Where to find: trees and bushes in woodland, scrub and gardens.

Feeds on: invertebrates, mostly flies.

Chameleons are famous for their remarkable ability to change colour. Their colour changes are primarily linked to emotion (e.g. fear, aggression and social signalling) via the nervous system, rather than camouflage. A message from the brain enlarges or shrinks special chromatophore cells under the top layer of clear skin, causing them to flush with colour pigments. This is similar to a human blushing. A chameleon's eyes are set within rotating turrets, formed by fused eyelids, and are unique in having the ability to move and focus independently of each other simultaneously. This affords the animal 180° vision on each side. Once prey has been located, both eyes focus on the same spot giving the animal a stereoscopic view and acute depth perception.

The chameleon fires its long tongue, armed with a sticky tip, at a speed which scientists have clocked at $1/30$th of a second. The insect is pulled into the mouth where it is immediately crushed and eaten. Although this happens far too quickly for the human eye to record, it sometimes makes an audible "*thwack*" on a leaf. The tong-like toes are fused in groups of two and three, and are equipped with sharp claws for climbing. This particular arrangement of toes, known as zygodactylic, is designed for clasping and is also common to parrots and woodpeckers – which, like the chameleon, are able to climb through foliage and up trunks.

What's in a name?
The scientific name derives from the Ancient Greek *chamae leo*, meaning 'dwarf lion', on account of its aggressive behaviour when threatened.

Striped Skink *Mabuya striata*

Swa: **Kasa** Maa: **Empur sambu**

Size: HBT 25 cm / 10"

Recognition: an attractive brown lizard with two cream stripes down the back.

Habits: basks on fallen trees and logs.

Where to find: wooded savanna and in the gardens of lodges and camps with fallen trees or rocks.

Feeds on: invertebrates such as grasshoppers and crickets.

In contrast to the dramatic agama lizards (*pages 140–141*), the skink is a slow and sedate reptile. It seeks food cautiously and with a stuttered motion, shoving its snout in the leaf-litter then pausing and awaiting the movement of a meal. Like the gecko species (*pages 138–139*), the Striped Skink can shed its tail when grasped by a predator, and stump-tailed skinks are a common sight. This skink is ovoviviparous, hatching their eggs internally and giving birth to live young.

Top tip: despite their amazing camouflage, chameleons can easily be found at night when their skin glows in torchlight.

Size: HBT 15 cm / 6"
Recognition: a noisy, bug-eyed lizard with rubbery skin.
Habits: nocturnal, chases bugs around lights at night.
Where to find: established buildings with electrical lighting.
Feeds on: small to large invertebrates and other geckos.

These nocturnal geckos are especially noisy and produce various clicks and chirps throughout the night as they socialise with other geckos. They are highly variable in colour and pattern. Their vertically-slit pupils are perfectly adapted for night vision. Like most other gecko species, the Tropical House Gecko lays two soft eggs in a crevice. The eggs harden quickly and are protected by the female.

Gecko Gadgets

They may be small and unobtrusive but geckos exhibit some amazing adaptations:

* The ability to run vertically, even upside-down, on smooth surfaces like glass, thanks to specialized toe pads on their webbed feet. Uniquely, this does not involve surface tension (as it does with small insects) but instead microscopic setae on the toe pads that apply attractive forces to the object on which they are walking.
* A quick-release tail that enables them to escape from predators, a function known as autotomy (see *opposite*).
* A lack of eyelids and the ability to clean their clear eye membranes by licking them with their long tongue.
* Parthenogenic females in some species, meaning they are capable of reproducing without copulating with a male.

Top tip: welcome these harmless lizards into your room as they kill bugs including mosquitoes.

Cape Dwarf Gecko *Lygodactylus capensis*

Swa: **Mjusi ndogo** Maa: **Empur**

Size: HBT 9 cm / 3½"

Recognition: a tiny lizard with round pupils and camouflaged colouration.

Habits: a daytime hunter of ants and small bugs; usually lives in trees but can become adapted to tents.

Where to find: common in and around camps and lodges.

Feeds on: small invertebrates.

The Cape Dwarf Gecko is smaller, slimmer and less noisy than Tropical House Gecko. Although they have adapted to tent poles and canvas, their natural habitat is mature forest, where small colonies are dominated by a single male, which shows a black throat. Approximately 60 species of dwarf gecko have been described, the vast majority from Africa, though more probably await discovery.

Autotomy This Cape Dwarf Gecko has successfully escaped predation by employing caudal autotomy (or 'tail self-severing', from the Latin *caudum* = tail and the Greek *auto* = self + *tomy* = severing). When under attack geckos, skinks and other lizards can shed their tail, which will wriggle and distract the predator while the animal escapes. The tail will partially regenerate (with cartilage replacing the original bone) over a period of a few weeks. Re-grown tails are often a different colour from the rest of the body.

Mwanza Flat-headed Agama
Agama mwanzae

Swa: **Mjusi kafiri**
Maa: **Olmokua oldo lukunya**

Size: HBT 32 cm / 12½"
Recognition: when displaying, males have a pink-red head, neck and back with a blue lower back and tail, turning mostly greyish-blue when relaxed. Females are predominantly brown with a pale neck and scattered white thorny scales.
Habits: basks on rocks to regulate body heat and to display, preferring to run under rocks when threatened.
Where to find: rocky outcrops and pathways, often close to water.
Feeds on: mostly ants, termites and other invertebrates, rarely small amphibians.

Red-headed Rock Agama
Agama agama

Swa: **Mjusi kafiri**
Maa: **Olmokua odo lukunya**

Size: HBT 35 cm / 14"
Recognition: when displaying, males are recognized by their peaked (not flat) head that is bright orange – the colour extending no further than the neck. The body and legs show turquoise-blue. It turns browner when relaxed but still shows an obvious pale stripe down the back that extends to the base of the tail. Females have many white spots on the head and body and usually show rusty-red stripes on the back.
Habits: basks on rocks to regulate body heat and to display, running underneath when threatened.
Where to find: common in rocky areas including cliffs and kopjes (outcrops).
Feeds on: mostly ants and other small invertebrates.

Female

Mwanza Flat-headed Agama

Male

Female

Male

Red-headed Rock Agama

Male

Agama drama

Agamas are medium-sized, long-tailed lizards that change colour according to their mood. Unlike chameleons, which show a range of colour variations, agamas are restricted to two combinations: bright and dull. Males are polygamous (*i.e.* they prefer more than one breeding partner, usually five or more) and highly territorial, resulting in great competition for females. Fighting often breaks out between competing males who will try to intimidate opponents with dramatic moves and open mouths. Once the 'boss' has been decided, he will court his delicate females with impressive head bobs and swings (think 'school disco'!). A female in the company of a shy male will wave her rear in front of him before running away until he catches up.

☐ Blue-headed Tree Agama
Acanthocercus atricollis

Swa: **Mjusi kafiri**
Maa: **Olmokua lorkeek**

Size: HBT 37 cm / 14½"

Recognition: when displaying, males are recognized by their vivid-blue head, turning browner when relaxed, with an obvious pale stripe down the back. Females have noticeable black patches on the collar.

Habits: basks on open ground to regulate body heat, running up trees or under bushes or rocks when threatened.

Where to find: open acacia country and short grass plains, where it is particularly fond of termite mounds, but also wooded savanna with clearings.

Feeds on: mostly ants, termites and other invertebrates, possibly small amphibians.

At least 37 species of *Agama* have been identified across Africa and many are similar in their behaviour and diet.

Top tip: be patient when trying to photograph lizards. If they run down a lair or up a tree, just sit comfortably nearby and wait for them to start showing off or feasting on the next passing ant swarm.

Black-necked Spitting Cobra *Naja nigricollis*   Swa: **Swilla**   Maa: **Olasurai Orok**

Size: HBT 2·7 m / 9 ft

Recognition: a slender black or dark-grey snake with wide bars of black and pink on the neck.

Habits: active day and night but most often encountered in the early morning.

Where to find: open and wooded savanna with plentiful termite mounds.

Feeds on: a wide variety of small mammals, reptiles and amphibians.

An attack is preceded by a threat display in which the snake inflates its neck into a hood by expanding its neck muscles. It also often raises its head up to 1 m / 3 ft off the ground for greater intimidating effect. However, the most dangerous cobra is one that bites, for this snake kills its prey with a potent cytotoxin that quickly breaks down the cells of its prey's organs and body tissue, causing a slow and painful death.

Although famed for its 'spitting' ability, this dangerous cobra doesn not actually 'spit' venom but 'shoots' it through tiny holes in the fangs. It is able to do so with exceptional accuracy within a 3 m / 10 ft range, usually aiming at the eyes of a threat or predator. It must be stressed that this is not a hunting technique but purely a defence mechanism, causing permanent blindness to untreated eyes; the venom is harmless on the skin.

If a Black-necked Spitting Cobra spits in the eyes of a Maasai, we cut the ear of a sheep and quickly put the blood in the eye. When we see a Cobra inside our Manyata (village), we place a bowl of milk near the entrance to lure it outside. It drinks the milk and then goes away.

Karipoi

Black Mamba *Dendroaspis polylepis*

Swa: **Koboko**   Maa: **Olasurai Ngioro**

Size: HBT 4 m / 13 ft

Recognition: a slender snake, usually olive-grey-brown in colouration with paler underparts. The pale coffin-shaped head contrasts with black beady eyes.

Habits: diurnal, usually located in trees but will sometimes travel along the ground.

Where to find: savanna and woodland, where it is fond of trees, termite mounds and other sites with protective bolt-holes.

Feeds on: a variety of mammals, birds and other reptiles, including snakes.

I was doing some grass research with colleagues at Ikoma when we set our study plot close to a road. As we started to unload our equipment we saw a Rattling Cisticola (a small warbler) flying over the Red Oat Grass giving its loud alarm call. We noticed movement in the grass and suddenly saw the head of a large Black Mamba raised up. We decided to stop and search for another study plot!   **Titus**

The Black Mamba gets its name from the ink-black colouration of the inside of the mouth and not its skin colour. Reaching lengths in excess of 4 m / 13 ft, this formidable predator is the longest venomous snake in Africa. It is very fast on the ground, often travelling on the rear half of the body alone, and is claimed by many to be the world's fastest snake, able to reach speeds of 20 kph / 12 mph. The Black Mamba has a reputation for attacking without provocation. Such attacks often involve female snakes protecting their eggs, and no mamba should be approached without an expert present.

The fast-acting venom contains a deadly mix of neurotoxins which affect the brain, and cardiotoxins that affect the heart and muscle tissue. Rarely, you may encounter two snakes writhing together in combat, which could be mistaken for mating behaviour.

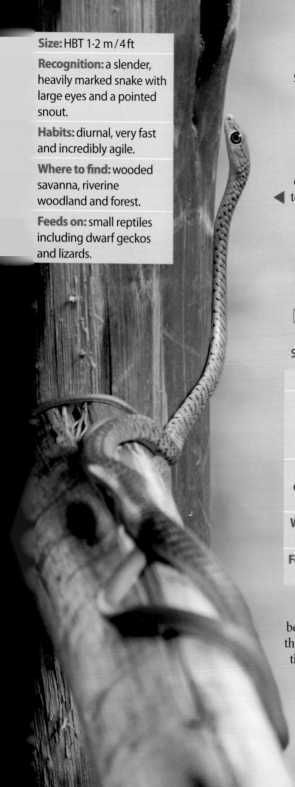

Size: HBT 1·2 m / 4 ft

Recognition: a slender, heavily marked snake with large eyes and a pointed snout.

Habits: diurnal, very fast and incredibly agile.

Where to find: wooded savanna, riverine woodland and forest.

Feeds on: small reptiles including dwarf geckos and lizards.

☐ Spotted Bush Snake
Philothamnus semivariegatus

Swa: **Nyoka ukuti**   Maa: **Olasurai onyori**

The Spotted Bush Snake is rarely seen on the ground as it prefers to hunt in trees and bushes. It is heavily scaled underneath, giving it excellent traction and it has been known to climb smooth tree trunks that appear to offer no grip at all. Of all the snakes the authors have encountered in East Africa, this one has the habit of turning up in the unlikeliest of places, including dining rooms and vehicle dashboards!

☐ Velvety-green Night Adder
Causus resimus

Swa: **Nyoka kijani**   Maa: **Olasurai onyori**

Size: HBT 70 cm / 28"

Recognition: a small but well-proportioned leaf-green snake with velvety-skin and small black flecks down the spine and flanks.

Habits: despite the name it is active day and night, but can be difficult to find in its woodland habitat.

Where to find: wooded savanna and riverine woodland.

Feeds on: mostly toads and frogs but also small invertebrates.

This attractive terrestrial snake may be encountered on trails and pathways through well-wooded areas. Bites from this snake are rarely recorded because it has adopted an impressive display to warn off threats. This involves inflating itself and hissing loudly, which is usually enough to draw attention and avoid people accidentally standing on it.

Puff Adder *Bitis arietans*

Size: HBT 1·9 m / 6 ft

Recognition: a fat-bodied and highly camouflaged snake, with a broad, triangular head.

Habits: sluggish, terrestrial and mostly nocturnal, when it lies in ambush or searches small holes for prey.

Where to find: open and wooded savanna, acacia scrub and forest edge.

Feeds on: mostly rodents and other small vertebrates.

The statistics speak for themselves: more people die in Africa from Puff Adder bites than from any other snake. However, unlike the Black Mamba (*page 143*), it is not an overtly aggressive snake and most attacks occur because the victim stands on one accidentally. This happens for three reasons: they are incredibly well camouflaged; they are reluctant to move when in danger; and they are mostly active at night when people tend to look ahead rather than at the ground. Like the Spitting Cobra (*page 142*), the venom is cytotoxic, causing similar cell malfunction. Unlike many other snakes, the Puff Adder moves in a straight line, caterpillar-fashion, rather than with a writhing motion.

African Rock Python *Python natalensis*

Swa: **Chatu** Maa: **Emeu**

Size: HBT 6 m / 20 ft

Recognition: a long, thick-bodied snake with a broad, spear-shaped head. The greyish, leathery skin is covered with brown and rusty patches of various sizes.

Habits: prefers to hunt at night but is often seen basking in the morning sun.

Where to find: a nomadic species that can be encountered in any habitat.

Feeds on: mammals up to the size of gazelle and, less frequently, birds and reptiles.

This is the largest snake in Africa, with specimens up to 9·8 m / 32 ft long being claimed in the central African forests – although the record length in East Africa measured 6 m / 20 ft. African Rock Python has very rarely been known to kill and eat humans. It locates its warm-blooded prey with heat-seeking pits on the snout and strikes with a fearsome mouth full of very sharp teeth. Once caught, the prey is immediately smothered by the coiling body of the snake and slowly crushed with an intensifying grip. Experts have suggested that the prey actually dies from a heart attack rather than suffocation. Pythons are able to unhinge their jaws to facilitate swallowing large animals, a process that can take many hours. Once inside the snake, prey can take many weeks, even months, to be digested and such well-fed beasts do not need to eat very often. Unusually among snakes, female pythons are fantastic mothers, guarding their eggs (up to 100, although 30 is more common) and later the hatchlings with vigilance for several weeks. It is thought that pythons are one of most primitive of all snake families as their skeletons possess vestigal limbs, suggesting they have not changed much from their earlier 'lizard days'.

I once encountered a huge Rock Python, almost 5 m (16½ ft) long, close to our camp in the northern Serengeti. It had recently died and in its stomach was a very large adult Bohor Reedbuck. I think it must have been interrupted or frightened by something and tried to regurgitate its meal, which must have caused severe and fatal problems. Remember that when large snakes have just eaten a big meal they are very vulnerable, so they should not be aproached too closely or be disturbed. **Albert**

When I was out grazing the cows on the border of the Serengeti and Maasai land, I went to dig some roots (ingeriol) for food. As I pulled one out from under a bush, I noticed it was actually some snake skin and quickly realized that I had just pulled the tail of a large python! My dogs were barking hysterically on the other side of the bush and as I went to have a look, there was another python eating a Dik-dik. **Karipoi**

Further reading and useful resources

Suggested further reading

A Field Guide to the Larger Mammals of Tanzania by Charles Foley, Lara Foley, Alex Lobora, Daniela De Luca, Maurus Msuha, Tim R. B. Davenport and Sarah Durant. Published in 2014 by Princeton **WILD***Guides*.

The Kingdon Field Guide to African Mammals by Jonathan Kingdon. Published in 2003 by Christopher Helm.

A Field Guide to the Reptiles of East Africa by Stephen Spawls, Kim Howell, Robert Drewes and James Ashe. Published in 2004 by Christopher Helm.

The Safari Companion: A Guide to Watching African Mammals by Richard D. Estes. Published in 2004 by Chelsea Green.

Eponym Dictionary of Mammals by Bo Beolens, Michael Watkins and Michael Grayson. Published in 2009 by John Hopkins University Press.

The anecdotes about the people who have mammals named after them were gleaned from this book. Like the companion volume to bird names, "Whose Bird?" it is a fascinating and highly recommended read.

Online resources

www.serengeti.org
The official website of the Serengeti National Park

www.ngorongorocrater.org
The official website of the Ngorongoro Conservation Area

www.tanzaniaparks.com
The official website of Tanzania National Parks, or TANAPA

www.elephantsandbees.com
This amazing project explores the use of African Honey Bees as a deterrent to African Elephants, thus reducing crop damage and conflict with people. Dr Lucy King and her team would really appreciate your support – so please log on and see what the buzz is all about!

www.tusk.org
Get involved with the organisation that is 'Protecting Wildlife, Supporting Communities, Promoting Education' in Africa.

For anyone seeking further inspiration about the joys of safari in Northern Tanzania, check out these wonderful blogs by two of the most experienced safari guides working in the region.

www.privileged-observer.blogspot.co.uk by Richard Knocker

www.ethan-kinsey.blogspot.co.uk by Ethan Kinsey

Acknowledgements

We are very grateful for the encouragement to produce this photographic guide from many friends and colleagues that we have met on the East African safari circuit over the years. But one group stands out above all others in terms of their enthusiasm for this project – the professional safari guides. They have been kind enough to share with us their intimate knowledge of the wildlife of this stunning region and their personal reflections on it. Among numerous others, this includes our 'Super Six' guides who so generously shared their Serengeti expertise with us and whose contributions greatly enrich this book: Albert Alfred Lucas and Petena Lukeine of Asilia Africa, and Karipoi Kisirito Ngaiseri, Mudy (Mohammed) Nuru, Patita Ole Maya and Titus Massay of &Beyond.

Wisdom and friendship also came from James Robertson (Kerr & Downey), Joe du Plessis (Asilia Africa), Niall Anderson and Leonie and Dale Wepener (&Beyond), Richard Knocker (Nomad), Clint Schipper (Kuro Expeditions) and Ethan Kinsey (Ethan Kinsey Safaris), for which we are greatly indebted.

For their friendship and unwavering support at all times, thanks go to our dear friends Tony and Betty Archer, Dudu (Deborah) Beaton, Lulu Keeble and Graham Roy, Ken and Michelle Dyball, Nigel Archer (Nigel Archer Safaris) and Mike Cheffings (Bateleur Safaris). For their warm hospitality and taking the very best care of us when on safari, we would also like to thank the following: Chris and Nani Schmeling at Kisima Ngeda – Lake Eyasi, Peter Kerr and team at Gibb's Farm, Jan Halfwerk and Gert Borst at Speke Bay Lodge. A special mention also to the team at Asilia Africa for their kindness and support during our visits to Dunia Camp (Serengeti) and Oliver's Camp (Tarangire) which we thoroughly enjoyed.

Our venture into Africa may never have been possible without the Fox family (Foxes African Safaris), especially Bruce and Jane who were brave enough to take a chance on us to manage their camps in southern Tanzania even though we had no prior experience at the time. The heads of the family, Geoff and Vicky Fox, were especially kind and helpful to us at their wonderful farm at Mufindi in the southern highlands and we shall always be grateful to them for the opportunities they opened for us.

Finally, to the team at **WILD**Guides: Rob Still, Andy and Gill Swash and Brian Clews (designer and editors and proof-readers extraordinaire) – you have once again weaved your magic to help us create something quite beautiful. We shall always be grateful for your hard work and diligence in bringing our vision to life. Thank you.

Photographic Credits

All the images included in this book were taken by the authors, Adam Scott Kennedy and Vicki Kennedy, apart from those listed below. We are very grateful to the following photographers for allowing their images to be reproduced:

Peter Bagnall (peterbagnall-wildlifeimages.co.uk): Wild Cat (*p. 38*).

Ian Beames (Ardea.com): Zorilla (*p. 52*).

Greg & Yvonne Dean (WorldWildlifeImages.com): Small-spotted Genet (*p. 40*); Slender Mongoose (*p. 48*); Aardvark (*p. 61*); Steinbuck (*p. 88*); Porcupine (*p. 113*); Patas Monkey (*pp. 120 & 121*).

Angus Hart (flickr.com/photos/angushart): Pangolin (*p. 60*).

Brian Scott (brianscottimages.com): Side-striped Jackal (*p. 55*).

Andy & Gill Swash (WorldWildlifeImages.com): Ngorongoro Crater (*p. 20–21*); Olduvai Gorge (*p. 22*) Grant's Gazelle (*pp. 12–13*); Spotted Hyena (*p. 43*); Hippopotamus (*p. 68*); Warthog (*p. 74*); Plains Zebra (*pp. 76–78*); Giraffe (*p. 81*); Eland (*p. 84*); Dik-dik (*p. 90*); Wildbeest (*pp. 105 & 106–107*); Grass Rat (*p. 111*); Blue Monkey (*p. 123*).

Warwick Tarboton (warwicktarboton.co.za): Bushpig (*p. 73*) Mountain Reedbuck (*p. 92*).

Index

This index includes the common English and *scientific* names of all the mammals and reptiles included in this book.

Common names in **bold** highlight the species that are afforded a full account.
Bold numbers indicate the page number of the main species account.
Blue numbers relate to other page(s) on which a photograph appears.
Normal black numbers indicate the page(s) where other mammal species are mentioned.